Transgender & Triggering The Life of Dylan Thomas Cotter

Transgender & Triggering The Life of Dylan Thomas Cotter

Dylan Thomas Cotter

Transgender & Triggering : The Life of Dylan Thomas Cotter

Cover Photo by: Dylan Thomas Cotter
Hair by: Dean Banowetz Hollywood Hair Guy®

Transgender & Triggering The Life of Dylan Thomas Cotter

About The Author:

Everyone loves an underdog. Dylan Thomas Cotter is a proud gay transgender activist, artist, author, motivational speaker, and publicist that resides in the Hollywood Hills with his partner. He is a former adult entertainer and has appeared in *Vice, Rolling Stone, Out Magazine, Pride.com, Yahoo! News, Mashable* and *Newsweek*. When you meet Dylan Thomas Cotter and hear his life story, you will understand why the words "amazing" and "inspiring" are often used to describe him.

Dedication:

To my Nan, for inspiring me to never give up and to keep learning something new every day.

To the love of my life Dean, thank you for loving me just as I am.

To my fellow trans community, for those who laid the foundation, so I could walk this path.

To the many charitable and nonprofit organizations that helped make my top surgery possible: *The Los Angeles LGBT Center, Queer Care, Angel Flight West, Gender Affirmative Letter Access Project, The National Council of Jewish Women - Los Angeles.*

To anyone who's fought through the darkness to find their light.

To those who will pick up this book one day and see themselves in it.

To those who seek out stories to help them understand the world.

To my TikTok community, for sharing your stories and support.

To my adult industry community, for connecting me with resources and work when I needed it the most.

To every single trans ally, thank you for standing with us.

To those who dare to be themselves in a world that desperately opposes them - my story is for you.

To everyone in my partner's life that has made an effort to get to know and be kind to me.

To myself, for not giving up.

TABLE OF CONTENTS

EARLY LIFE

LIFE IN HOLLYWOOD

EMPLOYMENT

HEALTHCARE

- Gynecologist

LESSONS & ADVICE

- Things I've Learned During My Transition
- What To Do If You're Not Selected by a Surgery Fund
- Being Your Own Success Story
- How I Handle Being Unappreciated
- Vision Boards
- Re-Examining My Blueprint of Love
- Am Writing (This Book)
- Life Lesson While Writing
- My Biggest Life Lesson
- Red Flags When Meeting New People - Creepy Men
- Having Unsupportive People in Your Life
- Transitioning and Jealousy - How I Manage People with Bad Vibes
- Transitioning and Envy

THOUGHTS

- My Thoughts on "Having" to Educate Cisgender People
- Haters Are Fans
- Why Pride Exists
- You're Not an Ally
- Trans Kids' Bodily Autonomy and My Experience as a Trans Man

- Trans Rights & Trans Erasure Attempts
- My Thoughts on the 2024 US Election
- Cis Men Stop Doing This It's Weird
- Lush An Exemplary Authentic Execution of Corporate Social Responsibility and Allyship

- Transitioning FTM Focused Products I've Used and my Thoughts
- Moving Thoughts

CLOSING

Introduction

Early Life

My name is Dylan Thomas Cotter. Proud and gay, I am a transgender man. I am forty-one years old as I write this book. I work as a publicist and live in the Hollywood Hills with my boyfriend. Formerly, I was an underwear model. I've also worked in the adult entertainment industry. My story has been featured in Vice, Rolling Stone, Out Magazine and other major media outlets.

I have persevered through bullying, suicidal thoughts, depression, transitioning, domestic violence, being shot at, experimenting with substances, enduring employment discrimination, living on the verge of homelessness, and managing C-PTSD. Eventually, I came out on the other side, building a personal brand, becoming a model and activist. To be clear, I never wanted to be anyone's inspiration—often wishing my life were easier—but that is simply my truth. I have made mistakes, just as we all do, and have put myself through many wild situations. Yet, like many others, I have overcome adversity. Additionally, I have helped build trans community programs, taught empowerment classes, and overseen LGBTQIA+ community advocacy groups. So yes, I've heard people call me an inspiration, but I never set out to be one. If sharing my story helps even one person, it is worth it. When you read this book, you'll see why 'amazing' and 'inspiring' are often words used to describe me.

This book contains explicit language and addresses domestic violence, suicide, and substance use. It is intended for adults only. If you are sensitive to these topics, my story may not be for you.

From an incredibly early age, I knew that the way I felt and the way society viewed me were not in alignment. Neighbors and family members would give me holiday gifts of dolls. I vividly remember looking up at my mother and saying sadly, "They don't really know me," then putting them down and walking up to my room to be alone. As a kid, when I felt sad, I would isolate myself as a coping mechanism. My deep-rooted sadness would soon become darker, and that is where my story begins, my first day of Catholic school at age six.

First Suicide Attempt at Age Six – Welcome to First Grade

The first time I tried to kill myself, I was six. It was my first day of first grade. For Catholic school, my mother laid my uniform on my bed. I looked sadly at the clothes as she knelt to eye level, disappointment on her face. "Can you make Mom a deal?" she asked. "Wear this to school, and when you get home, you can wear whatever you want. Can you do that for Mom?" We didn't know about trans people at the time. "Yes," I answered. She smiled and closed the door, allowing me to get changed. At six, I didn't have the words to know it was possible to be transgender. Looking at the red checkered jumper, white blouse, and knee socks, my first thought was that I wanted to die.

I wanted the feeling to stop, and my first impulse was to kill myself. I grabbed a knee sock, wrapped it around my neck, and pulled hard to cut off my air. After several seconds, I knew it wouldn't work. I tossed the sock on the bed, sighed, glanced at the jumper, and got dressed.

Every time I wore a jumper or dress after that, I remembered. My coping mechanism became dissociation. I became skilled, especially as a child, at acting as if everything was fine when it wasn't, because I knew once I got home from school, I wouldn't have to wear a dress.

What I Wanted to Be When I Grew Up

When we are little kids, we often get asked: What do you want to be when you grow up? Let me set the scene—I was in Brownies, my mother signing me up as a precursor to Girl Scouts. One day, after school, the troop leader asked us what we wanted to be and told us to draw it and present our ideas. I was excited because I loved to draw. When she called my name, I went up with my drawing. She frowned, looked confused, said my deadname, and asked who I drew and what I wanted to be. I took the drawing, showed everyone, and said I wanted to be Magic Johnson. She told me, 'Girls do not play basketball.' That hurt, especially since I was obsessed with basketball. Years later, I shared this story with an Uber driver and talked about being a trans man. He replied, 'Well, it seems like you're your own magic at this point.' That made me smile; while I'm not Magic Johnson, I've found my own magic by becoming who I truly am. Still, Magic Johnson remains my favorite basketball player and a significant role model.

The Black Sheep

Growing up as the black sheep, I am proud to break generational toxic family systems. My large family includes many aunts, uncles, and cousins—my father is one of seven children and my mother one of six. Yet, I do not take part in that family ecosystem, and I will explain how this relates directly to my immediate family.

Before I was even brought into this world, I was not a fan of my father. Now you see, I can say that because when my mother was pregnant with me, the joke that has been told my entire life, which the other finds funny, is that my mom had to call him. He was down the street at a neighbor's party, and he was drunk the first six years of my life. My father was a big alcoholic. And so, I am trying to come into this world as a little baby, and I already can feel my mother's stress. And so, she gets him, he drives her drunk to the hospital, and she has me.

I am a Capricorn rising, so I am serious as fuck, and this is what shaped me as a child. I never wanted to be around my dad. I never wanted him to hold me or anything like that. The only times we got along were when he was drunk because he would make jokes. And I thought, you know, because I was a little kid, that he was going to be my buddy.

And then once he stopped drinking, he was resentful, and he would come home, and he would be like, What did you learn from school today? And this and that, and he would verbally take out all his things on me. As a child, I would call out jokes made about distinct types of people. I would say we do not talk about people like that. I remember checking on him at seven years old in a grocery store about the comments he had made. I grew up around homophobic jokes that were hurtful because I knew I was different. When I started to realize as a teenager, I started to get mad, and I was like, Do not say that shit around me. And so here I am, a proud trans gay man, and that is his karma.

I grew up quite differently from my brothers. I am one of three children; I am also the middle child. I am not the golden child at all. I am the scapegoat, and my father is a narcissist. Anything I wanted to do with my life or that I aspired to be was dismissed and second-guessed.

The summer after high school, my dad said, "You've got two weeks, find a full-time job or get the fuck out." I was eighteen and didn't know how to respond. My brothers weren't treated this way, which is why I won't visit them.

So, fast forward six months, and I realize I want to go to college. Would you like to look at a college with me? And my dad takes me to look at a college in Philadelphia. We lived in New Jersey at the time, and we came back home, and I am happy because I want to go there. And he says, "You know, I am not going to sign any of those FAFSA forms. You are not going there." And I say, "What?" He says, "No, I'm not going to help you." I did not want him to pay for anything. I just wanted him to fill out these forms because, at 18 years old, I didn't really understand how the world worked yet. And so, I thought I could not do anything at that point. And I was mad.

I thought to myself, Why would he dangle something in front of my face like that? And I was like, "Okay, so a year later, I took out a bunch of loans." One day, I said to my father, "You know, I'm moving to California," and he exploded, shouting at me in anger. I was like, yeah, I need to get away from this toxic environment, and so I got away from it. But did I ever escape it for the next twenty years? No, and I no longer speak to my father or my mother.

I will say that my older brother was always praised for every activity he undertook, and my parents made sure to let me know about every move he made. My father would constantly call me in college and start talking to me about my older brother. And I would say I do not need to talk about him, and at the same time, he was always updating me on my brothers; I was never asked about myself. My younger brother lives with my family to this day. So that "oh you've got two weeks to find a full-time job or get the fuck out of my house" did not really apply to him, but I love my younger brother. So, I am glad he was not treated the way that I have been.

I am confident that I was put on this earth to shake things up, but I never signed up to be treated so wildly differently, whether as a child or an adult. My father always desperately sought the approval of his mother, who was always trying to change him. And that is the one thing my father's been trying to do, is change me my whole life, and I have never put up with that and never will. Just because you are blood does not mean you are family, from my life experience. I always tell people the best thing you can do is be yourself. I understand what it is like to grow up and feel like you can't, and be surrounded by people who make fun of you or make fun of those who are like you, and those are the people who are supposed to love you.

The real people in your life who are your family will love you for exactly who you are. I'm proud to be nothing like my father. During the pandemic, I was struggling to make ends meet, and I was receiving phone calls from my father, my sister-in-law, my mother, and my brother because they were all arguing over the colors of party plates. So clearly, we live in two vastly different worlds, and I no longer entertain any of them. I speak with my younger brother here or there, but there's never an effort that has been put in on my family's end towards me unless they need, want something, or are trying to take credit or align themselves with something I've accomplished without their help or support, so it's a disappointment, but it is what it is.

I have been told by people important in my life that if he knew better, he would do better. But when you can see that someone is actively unwilling to unlearn their toxic behaviors, it is ok to remove yourself from that situation. I no longer feel an obligation towards any of them, and I have explained this to my mother. Growing up in a household where you are treated very differently from your siblings can make you feel, on some level, when you are younger, that you deserve it. And if that is happening with anyone, or you just know that you do not deserve it, and when you do your deep healing, you will see that it was not your fault. There will be some relief, and there will be some sorrow, but the best thing is not to continue that cycle.

If I ever had kids, I would never treat them the way I was treated. However, I am quite into astrology, and my birth chart and the circumstances of my birth are not typical for many people. I can see it has deeply shaped my personality and made me go, "Oh, ok, you don't think I can do that? Watch me. Oh, you don't believe in me? Ok. Well, I believe in myself." The best thing I can tell people is to always believe in themselves. If you take away anything from me, I hope it is this one thing.

Being Bullied and Suicidal

We moved from New Jersey to Virginia, where I was bullied for my clothes during my first two years of Middle School. I dreaded the school bus because neighborhood kids immediately called me "sweatpants." They had no idea I was simply ahead of the athleisure curve, but that was okay.

Towards the end of my first year of daily torment, as I exited the bus and walked home, my next-door neighbor called me "sweatpants" behind my back and laughed with my older brother, who had allowed his friends to bully me for nearly a year and joined in their laughter. Little did his ignorant friend know what he was in for that day.

After he called me names, I threw down my backpack and, channeling my inner Joe Pesci, yelled, "That's it!" I charged at my bully and beat him up as my older brother watched and stopped laughing.

As the first year of middle school ended and my next-door neighbor graduated, I thought the bullying would not continue the next year. I was wrong. On the first day of my second year of middle school, one of my bullies' younger brothers greeted me on the bus by yelling "sweat-pants" at me. He later signed up for my co-ed soccer team, where he un-successfully tried to bully me. I then quite successfully went ahead and took every available opportunity to slide tackle the ball out from under him in practice – much to his embarrassment.

The bullying continued during school hours, on the bus, and at other events. At the school dance, I was again relentlessly taunted and ended up pushing my bully to the ground for all to see. "Don't Speak" by No Doubt blared and echoed off stacked tables in the cafeteria. I stood my ground as he laughed, got up, and walked away. In my second year of bullying, I stared at my pink disposable razors at night, often considering ending it. But I thought about my mom and didn't want her to go through that. I was so happy when my parents told us we would be moving. I hated middle school, and my older brother never had my back, often thinking it was acceptable to befriend my bullies.

Boys Don't Cry

Ok, look, I had no idea someone could even be transgender until one afternoon when I was 16 years old, the trailer for BOYS DON'T CRY rolled across my small color TV. "So, you're a boy now, what?" alone in my room, my head snapped back like a rubber band to watch the full trailer. My life would never be the same. Instantly, I knew – oh fuck that is me. I mean, it is not me, but it, it fucking is, you know? I had to see this movie. I had to figure some shit out. Now, living as a teenager in southern New Jersey, I was not about to let anyone find out how I was feeling. I knew I had to watch this movie, and I had to keep it a secret. Not one person.

My adolescent mind was flooded with ideas on how I would get my hands on a copy. First, I thought, Blockbuster! Nope. Fuck. Can't do that. It's Mom's account; she'll be able to see it. Hmmm... ok, I'll buy it! Wait. Where are they selling this? It is not your typical Jersey flick. Few places in suburban New Jersey had it in stock at the time. Then I thought... Suncoast! A film geek's paradise located right in the Moorestown Mall. If anyone has it, it will likely be them. I gassed up my beige 1996 Mercury Sable, bumped some Jimmy Eat World, and was on my way to the mall. As I strolled through the food court in my bright yellow Independent Trucks hoodie and oversized navy cargo pants, Vans skate shoes (always on the cusp of fashion), a sense of both calmness and anticipation came over me.

My entire life, I'd felt different without knowing why. The chance to watch a movie based on a real trans experience was thrilling, even though I didn't grasp the whole story from the trailer. Nothing had prepared me for seeing Brandon Teena's story unfold—the violence was a shock I'd never forget. While not the ideal introduction to trans culture, it was important. My research into myself, however, took a turn when I ran into some guys from high school at the store. Two worked the counter. Panic set in, but I decided I wouldn't leave without that tape. Thanks to baggy cargo pants, I managed to sneak the tape out. Deep breath. Here we go.

Walking through the aisles of VHS releases, I kept my eyes on the exit, noticing every slight movement of the tape hidden in my left pocket. "Keep it moving," I told myself. Passing the front counter, adrenaline fluttered in my chest. Seconds from the entrance and security system, I wasn't sure if I'd set it off. Staying cool outwardly while panicking inside, I thought, "Well fuck it. Here we go." My worn skate shoes hit the mall's white tile floors. I exhaled. Omg. I did it. I fucking did it!

Now, let us fast-forward to the present day. Morally, as a 41-year-old man, I have remorse about stealing. It is the antithesis of what I believe to be honorable. We all make mistakes, deserve second chances, and can learn to be better people. What I do not at all have remorse for is seeking to learn through the only example I felt was a possibility at the time. Desperate times, people. Desperate times. Could you please let me know where to send the check? After watching BOYS DON'T CRY, it would take me exactly another sixteen years until I had the courage and frankly had gone through enough fucking garbage in life to move forward with my physical transition. The next section explores two relationships from this period that would significantly shape and impact my interactions in terms of sex, love, and dating.

After High School: The Family Showdown and Moving to California

My father and I had visited The Art Institute of Philadelphia, where I had hoped to attend college for video production. Upon returning home to New Jersey, about twenty minutes outside of the city, my father let me know he would not be filling out the FAFSA. I did not understand how any paperwork worked at the time, and I was confused because I would be taking out the loans on my own. But I should have known he would not help me figure things out. You see, my father has and continues to have a pattern of saying one thing and doing another. I remember many nights as a child sitting home and waiting on the steps in the dark for my Dad to come home and play football with me like he had promised only for him to either not show up because he was at the bar, or take me with him to the bar instead where my mother would later have to come to pick me up from (with tears in her eyes from crying about) or when he would show up sometimes rather than tell me no, he just walk right by me and not say anything.

After eighteen years of being an afterthought, I had reached my breaking point and made a promise to myself that one way or another, I would not just settle for attending school in Philadelphia; I was going to make movies in Los Angeles. So, a few months passed after high school had ended, and one afternoon, my father turned to me and said, in a calm voice, "You have two weeks, get a full-time job or get the hell out of my house." Now you see my dad never spoke to my brothers this way. He paid for some of my older brother's education. I always felt, considering his relationship with his mother and my mother, that he has issues with women, as if you were not a woman who just went along with everything, he thought he would either tune you out or speak down to you for not allowing yourself to be controlled. After he said what he said, I looked at him and said "Ok" and then I did what I did. I secured a full-time position as a manager at a larger athletic footwear retailer. I saved up my money for one year. I bought a used car (that my dad would later sell without my permission when I was out of town). I took out college loans to cover the costs of my move and education. When I told him, he was livid, and I was ready to get out of his house. He ended up flying out to California to help me get settled in, and I was sad when he left. Looking back, I would do it all over again; however, I could have done without the less-than-treatment compared to my brothers throughout our childhood.

LIFE IN HOLLYWOOD

Sex, Violence, and C-PTSD

Now, look, I could not have written this book without laying down the proper foundation. It will come up later, thankfully, in a more awkwardly humorous way. This is a tough chapter. That said, if you are triggered by domestic violence, you have been warned.

Unfortunately, my two most significant romantic relationships were violent. I experienced violence with both partners, more than once. Talking about it isn't easy, so I'll give you the Cliff's notes, as this topic could fill a book on its own. At nineteen, I moved from New Jersey to Los Angeles before transitioning. My first cisgender heterosexual boyfriend in college would put me down verbally, and when I resisted, the anger escalated. This ended with him punching me in the face in 2003 over a disagreement. Writing this in 2024, the body memory still lingers; my face hurts every time I recall it. Despite this, we stayed in an unhealthy relationship for three years.

It ended after a party where I wanted to leave, and he didn't. Imagine attending a party with someone who trashed half the guests to you, only to act friendly around them—it was uncomfortable and tiring. I eventually convinced him to leave by falsely promising sex. At home, I admitted my exhaustion and asked to sleep instead. He lost it, cursing at me, and then attacked when I told him off—busting my lip and throwing me down on the futon, pinning me painfully. He was far bigger and stronger, and he forcefully held me down.

This time, I truly feared for my life. I yelled, spat in his face, and kicked him, which gave me a split second to escape to the kitchen. The studio apartment, though small and tacky, happened to have a door I could lock. He pounded and screamed insults while I cried, cleaned my bloody mouth, and curled up next to the refrigerator for the night. That was my first boyfriend—let's call him "Mr. Wonderful."

Cutting, Drinking, and Falling Down in Hollywood

After going back to live in New Jersey for a few months following the horrific end of my relationship, I moved to West Hollywood. I got a job at a studio expendables store and made a group of work friends (looking back, more so drinking friends). In the span of a few short years, I got to know and drink at most every bar and strip club in Hollywood and West Hollywood. Never having been a drinker in college, there was absolutely a learning curve that took place. I was lucky I had the friends I did because, unknowingly, I was drinking to avoid my sexuality and gender identity. So heavily so that I would drink until I would either blackout and continue functioning or just pass out altogether. I was drinking myself to numb the pain I had from the breakup, to avoid exploring my sexuality, which kept coming up. On the nights I could not find someone to go out with, I started drinking at home. To combat the moments where I felt disconnected from my body, I started cutting myself.

I would go as long as I could until I started feeling too much, then I would bandage myself up, throw on a long-sleeve shirt, and hit the nearest bar. The Coach and Horses was my go-to at the time. One night, I remember walking in and sitting down with my friend Jim. A guy came right up to us and called me by my deadname (I was still presenting as female at the time). "I really enjoyed our conversation the other night". I nodded, smiled at him, and turned to my friend Jim, mouthing, "I don't remember." It seemed that during my whiskey streak, I liked to go into the Coach and Horses and get tanked, yet still be able to hold eloquent conversations about life. I was a ticking time bomb, a true functioning train wreck waiting to happen. My twenties were wild and rough, and I am glad this was right before social media became as popular as it is today. My cutting and heavy drinking slowed down after my friend Jim saw me lift my sleeve one night and laid into me. We still partied, but no longer on that level. I could see I scared him, and that scared me.

Cocaine and Chemo

My father called me one day while I was mildly hungover at work. I was jolted back into reality when I heard him crying—my father never cries. He told me my brother was in the hospital with leukemia and that I needed to get on a plane, to be ready if they needed bone marrow from a sibling. My younger brother and I were his best chance. I took the call in the back break room, sobbing because I was terrified for my brother—and because I felt like a horrible human being.

You see, I was not just hungover from drinking; I had very recently started to experiment with Cocaine. I knew I couldn't save him because I wouldn't pass the test. I found out my brother was fighting for his life while I had been recklessly throwing mine away. We are lucky he ended up not needing bone marrow. We are lucky that if he did, my younger brother was not as much of a fuck up as I was in my 20s. I have never and will never touch the stuff again. I no longer speak with my older brother, but if I got a call that he needed a marrow transplant now, and if I were a match, I would be ready and willing to help him out, although I doubt he'd return the favor.

You Never Know

A good friend of mine and I were really into punk rock. One day, she sent me a link to a music video for "Thrash Unreal" by Against Me! When I looked at the then pre-transition Laura Jane Grace, I instantly thought to myself, "That is exactly what I want to look like." I did not dare say anything because I was not out yet. Years later, I discovered that Laura Jane Grace had also transitioned. The lesson: You never truly know what kind of story someone is living. I am a believer that, in some way, in the universe, all our energy is connected.

Coming Out & Binding

When I look at my dating history, I feel like my first girlfriend and I had a lot of fun together. We were together for about three and a half years. What I both loved and disliked about her was that she pushed me to grow, and sometimes, when I was not ready. We had been living together for a few months; she gave me an ultimatum - come out to my family or our relationship was over. Looking back on it now, I get why she felt the way she did; however, I would have handled it differently had I been in her shoes.

I ended up writing an email to my parents. I remember I was wearing a bright Kelly-green polo shirt (so gay) and crying when I hit the send button from my office in Beverly Hills. It was fine, they did not seem to mind. I was scared at the thought of losing them; I was also scared at the thought of losing her. It was a tough time. Later in our relationship, she kept nagging me about going shopping for bras, which I kept avoiding. I remember she came into the dressing room with me at Sears, and I had a tearful breakdown and was just being so sad about my body. At that moment, she was great. She could tell I was not happy with my body, and so she asked me if I would feel better if my chest were flat. I said yes, and she instantly took charge, saying, 'Okay, we are going home, we are looking at binders, and we are getting you what you need to feel good.'

We did just that, and I remember the first day my binders arrived in the mail. After I figured out how to use them, I had the biggest smile because I felt and looked more like I was supposed to. Our love story ended in what would be yet another devastating heartbreak for me. We had decided to give Santa Fe, New Mexico, a shot and move from Los Angeles. We had visited many times before, as it was her hometown. We had been experiencing problems on and off for months and thought that moving could be the solution to our issue. That would prove to be false. After being there for only two weeks and living with her family, we were no longer speaking. Without a job to keep me busy or friends to hang out with, I felt isolated. I needed to see my family. I booked a one-way ticket and told her I would book a trip back after spending some time with my family.

She took me to the airport two days later, we kissed, I told her I would see her soon, and we kept in regular contact. At the end of two weeks, I told her I was going to book my ticket back – she told me not to. I was confused. Then I was not. Then I was heartbroken. I did not think we would ever break up, and in the process, I lost all my possessions. I would then spend the next six months staying with my parents in New Jersey and sleeping on a couch in their rented condominium. I moved back to Los Angeles.

My Second Girlfriend: The Brief Beginning of a Long Seven Years Together

We met on Craigslist, and she was gorgeous. We met when she was on vacation in Hawaii, and I was visiting my parents in New Jersey. We immediately started video chatting. We would end up chatting for six months before I moved back out to Los Angeles. We hooked up the same day my flight got in and hung out for a good solid two weeks until she told me she was getting back together with her girlfriend. I was sad, but I asked if we could stay friends, and she said no. I said OK and that I understood. I smiled and waved as she drove away, and our paths would cross again later.

The Hate Crime

Of all the things that have happened in my life, I feel that having my life threatened and being shot at has changed me the most. After moving back to Los Angeles, a high school friend and I rented a live/work loft in Echo Park for our startups. He stayed in Oregon, leaving me living and working there alone. Echo Park, on LA's east side, is densely populated. Longtime residents resented newcomers, particularly those, like myself, who were visibly queer.

It was a dreary Spring afternoon; I had gotten back together with my girlfriend and was excited as I got off the bus to come home to my new baby puppy, Chiweenie named Ducky. Ducky was my best friend, and while I felt at the time that I had no idea if any of my work ventures would be successful, I knew that being Ducky's dad was the most successful and fulfilling experience I had ever had.

Eager to hang out with my little buddy, I entered the property from Sunset Blvd., I walked up the alleyway on the side of the building, and unlocked the door to the exterior spiral staircase. As I tried to make my way up. I saw a younger-looking gangster (in his 20s) sitting on top of his car, drinking alone in the parking lot diagonally across from the staircase steps from my unit's front door. "Hey, you fucking faggot!" he yelled in a thick accent. My heart dropped into my stomach. I thought to myself, oh fucking of course, now I am going to pass to someone who is a homophobe. "I'm gonna fucking kill you!" he yelled again and laughed as I continued to keep my head down, exiting the staircase, unlocking my front door, and locking it quickly behind me. My life at that building was never the same again from that moment, and I knew in that instant that it never would be.

At night, all the neighborhood gangsters would come to the parking lot that was located diagonally outside of my loft. Over the fence, they throw Big Gulps full of ice and soda at my back glass patio doors. My puppy would get so scared that she would pee herself as she ran to hide in the bathroom. It progressed into having bullets shot into the back of my unit. Thankfully, it missed the back patio's glass doors; otherwise, I would not be writing this right now. I would call the police nightly and they would say the same thing. Stay inside, do not leave your unit, and we will send someone out. I was powerless, afraid, and knew I needed to get Ducky out of there fast.

While this was all happening, the startups were taking longer than my business partner had expected and were not generating any return on investment. It was not something that he or I had financially planned on. I did not have the money to take over the lease alone, and even if I had, it was not a safe option. The decision was clear: I would either have to move back to New Jersey, or my girlfriend and I could move in together. Of course, I was madly in love with her at the time, and she cared for me; however, we never initially moved in together out of love. She always reminded me of that, and that I was living in her apartment. That was an absolute shitty feeling, but I was grateful for what I thought was out of harm's way. Little did I know of the challenges ahead of us from living together.

Alone Together

I had just been recruited for an exceptionally large corporate strategy position. It was created for me to help bridge the gap between a major motion picture equipment rental supplier and its parent company (an international car rental chain) for their UK expansion. My then-girlfriend and I, at the time, were living together in Glendale, and this was great news, as it meant we wouldn't have to endure the daily Hollywood traffic commute (and especially since we were sharing a car). We were excited because I'd be making way more money than ever. We had been struggling and not getting along, so I thought that having more money and this job would bring us closer together. Things did not exactly go that way.

My then-girlfriend was still heavily drinking at the time. I was working full-time and would be exhausted by the time I got home. She was working part-time at night and was staying out drinking after work. I felt like I was not getting to see her, and we would talk about it. She made it clear that she did not want to stop going out, and I made it clear that I felt like I was alone in the relationship. One night, after we had a text disagreement while she was out, I went to sleep because I had work the next morning. Around about 2:30 am, I was woken up by having my hair pulled and dragged out of bed. Yes. She came home drunk, was pissed, and violent. After I stood up and looked at her, I could see how drunk she was and that there was no use in arguing with someone that far gone. She continued to call me every nasty name in the book, while she began hitting me, she continued verbally putting me down in the most hurtful ways she knew would affect me deeply. Comments about me needing to "man up", etc. At first, I was shocked, and then I became incredibly sad. I cried for hours and slept for two before having to get up and go into my very corporate job.

I went into work the next morning, exhausted, bags under my puffy, bloodshot eyes from crying for hours the night before. Some of the girls in the office assumed I had gotten very stoned the night before and tried to crack some jokes with me. I bit my tongue, put on a fake smile, and laughed as I closed my office door. I cried in my office that afternoon and left at 6 pm wearing my sunglasses. People can assume what they want and often will, but can never truly know what someone else is going through. The next morning, rather than walk to my car to drive to work, I walked to the side of the freeway on-ramp. I sat crying on the side of the road in Glendale, wanting to run into traffic. Not wanting to go in and have them be so tone-deaf as to assume that I was a 24/7 stoner when, in reality, my then-girlfriend was beating me up. I called out that day, saying I had food poisoning. It was an incredibly sad walk back home that afternoon.

Living in a Motel – Two Weeks Away from Homelessness

After nine long months in my corporate position, I quit. My partner's mother was living in the desert, and we decided to move in with her while we looked for jobs. Living in the Palm Desert/Palm Springs area initially sounded like a great idea. Once we arrived, the novelty soon wore off when we realized how scarce job opportunities were. After living with my partner's mother and her mother's boyfriends for a few months, we were all not getting along very well. My partner decided it was time for us to leave, considering we had little money and not much consistent work. So, we moved into a Travelodge in Cathedral City, California, where my partner, our dog, and cat all shared a single motel room. We had reached a new low.

Every day, I would look for work while my partner worked part-time at a furniture store. Every night that she would come home from work, she would start drinking, and the pattern of her verbally ripping into me about how much of a failure I was would eventually be the topic of conversation. One night, she went right to the nearby bar instead of coming home. I couldn't get in touch with her for hours and was worried. Eventually, she showed up completely drunk. I was not happy, and I let her know. She flew into a violent rage, yelling at me, calling me a loser, and hitting me. I kept telling her to stop, and eventually she tired herself out enough and passed out on the bed. Ten minutes later, I hear her coughing as she lies on her back. She was vomiting and choking. Terrified, I rushed to her and turned her over. The entire ordeal was horrific. She threw up all over the bed. I carried her into the tub, and she moaned at me like she was still mad. Here I was trying to help her, and she was fucking angry with me. It was so God damn exhausting.

She cried and threw up as I bathed her in the tub. When I finally got her back into bed, I made sure she had water and empty bags around the bed in case she had to throw up again. To this day, it is one of the lowest points of my life. I did not know how either of us would be after this. That week, I was fortunate enough to secure a gig as a social media marketer for an entertainment industry SaaS startup. The pay was enough for us to at least stay afloat in the motel, which I was grateful for, because the night she got sick, we were about two weeks away from having to live in our van. We would later be able to move back to Los Angeles with the financial help of her mother; however, our relationship was strained and never the same.

Other Violent Relationship

My other relationship, which also took a violent turn, I feel more physiologically affected me on a deeper level. The curveball is that it was with a cisgender woman. Yes, I wasn't attracting the best situations for most of my twenties and early thirties. I was with my ex-girlfriend for a total of seven years, and I loved her madly. I say madly because no matter what she did or said, I could not get enough of her. Goddammit. I was fucking addicted to her, and she was addicted to alcohol. During that time, we both had a lot of things happening, but when we met, I told her, "You know I am going to transition; I don't know exactly when, but it is going to happen." She told me she was cool with it because she was bisexual, and so that was that, or so I thought.

Working in a hyper-masculine industry, being perceived as a lesbian when I never identified as one, I already stuck out, and I just felt like I could not deal with the stress of transitioning on the job and coming out to my family. For many years, I was sad all the time. And when I was sad, I drank. I drank to feel happy, and my ex and I had drinking in common until I started getting sick from it. Then it was no longer fun, and to her, it started to feel like I was no longer fun. When the drinking dynamic between us changed, we both started looking at each other differently. I didn't want to go out, and she wanted to party. She would get frustrated, and I would not be as attracted to her when she had one too many; that is when she started to turn from a funny drunk to a mean drunk. The difference between Mr. Wonderful and her when they got violent was just that to me – gender.

You see, when Mr. Wonderful would come at me, I would physically defend myself. With her, I just could not. I loved her too much and would just always repeat to myself in my mind, "she has no idea what she's doing," not to justify her actions, but more to say that she has no idea how this is fucking me up on so many levels. I had already been through the violence with my monster of a college boyfriend, and when my ex-girlfriend would hit me, it would trigger the body memories from before, and in the situation with her, I felt I could not do anything to defend myself. I would freeze, and I would take it because I never wanted to be the type of guy my college boyfriend was. I never wanted to put my hands on a woman.

The other reason this relationship caused me deep physiological damage was because, you see, I was a little kid, and my dad was an alcoholic. He has been sober for over thirty years. Also important to note is that my dad was never violent with my mom, me, my brothers, or anyone else. Aside from the violent occurrences from my ex-girlfriend's drinking, it would trigger not-so-great childhood memories. Memories of my mom not knowing where my dad was because he did not come home – I was now living my mom's experience when my then-girlfriend would not come home. I would get so stressed and freaked out, not knowing where she was and worrying if she was ok. I expressed all this to her, and drinking took priority - always. It magnified my pain on so many fucked up levels.

It all came to a head one night after she came home from work. Her routine would be to call me on her way back from work every night and complain about most of the hour ride back. It was hard on my soul. It stressed me out, but she never noticed those signals, and she would get mad at me when I flat-out told her she was stressing me out. I felt like I could not win. When she got home, she would go straight for a drink, spend the entire evening on Instagram or watching HGTV, and not want to talk to me before judging me for not doing something or just putting me down in some way, before going to bed. It was a sad, vicious cycle, and I felt lonely in the sixth year of our relationship.

After some time, I grew tired and started sleeping on the couch. That evening, I was especially frustrated after a phone call. Knowing I'd face more negativity when she came home and opened the tequila, I hid it. When she returned and spent time searching, she asked where it was. I lied—I simply didn't want another miserable night. I hated going to bed feeling bad. She didn't believe me, kept searching, and became angrier, cursing at me. I held the lie for about ten minutes as she got more upset. The scene became both scary and childlike, like a toddler's tantrum. It was truly unattractive and deeply sad to realize my feelings mattered less than her alcohol.

When I finally caved and pulled the bottle out from underneath the sink, she fucking lost it. She pushed me back and kept coming forward, hitting me with her fists, cursing at me. And again, I just took it, but this time I kept telling her, "Stop! You don't know what you're doing! You don't know what you're doing!" That pissed her off even more. I moved past her into the hallway and then locked myself in the bathroom. The scenario felt eerily like the one with Mr. Wonderful. She was yelling at me to come out and to move out.

I came out of the bathroom and asked her to stop screaming because I did not want the neighbors to call the cops, but she hit me again. "Ok, well, should I call the cops?" she said. "You go ahead and call them. Who do you think they're going to believe? Someone who looks like you or looks like me?" Now, what you must understand is that, as wild as she was behaving, she had a point. She is a blonde woman with great skin and a soft voice; she exudes charm when she wants to. I was just a queer guy with a bunch of tattoos who was not yet on testosterone. I was terrified of going to jail, and she knew that, and that sucked.

The next day, I moved in with a marketing client of mine. I had no "friends" in Los Angeles who would let me stay on their couch. The only thing I will say is that it is amazing how much you can be there for others and how they can turn a blind eye when you need them most. I lived with my client for about three months. Long story short, my next roommate ended up being a magician who was bipolar and not a fan of taking his medication – it was a dire situation, so scary in fact that I went back to living with my ex for a few months. Like an idiot, I got hooked on her again, and we decided that I would find an apartment down the street so we could share our dog and work things out, eventually getting back to living together.

I know! I know how bad that sounds now, but at the time, I was oblivious—just happy and in love. One day, I went to pick up our dog Ducky. Opening the door, I was struck by a sick feeling in my gut—a sharp shift from moments before. I had never gone through her stuff, but that day I did. I flipped open the laptop. Skype was open, and a message popped up: 'Marv: I miss you.' I slammed it closed. What. The. Actual. Fuck. I called her; she answered, cheerful as ever. "Hey, babe! What's up?" I asked in my calmest voice, "Who is Marv and why the fuck does he miss you?" Silence. I repeated, angrier, "Who the fuck is Marv, and why does he miss you?" She blurted, "He's a family friend." Now pissed, I said, "Yeah, right. Facebook is for family friends, Skype isn't." I hung up, dropped my key on the coffee table, hugged Ducky goodbye, and locked the door behind me.

I started walking, called a friend, and had her stay on the phone with me until I got to Akbar, where I continued to get very, very drunk. I do not remember how I got home that evening, but thankfully, I did and in one piece. My seven-year relationship was over. I was devastated. She had been seeing a cisgender guy and lying to me. It was deeply hurtful.

Less than a year later, she called me crying. Worry and old pain surged. The same guy she left me for had beaten her, and she had kicked him out. I ran down the street. Relief and sadness collided as I hugged her. I sat with her as she described his abuse. It was the saddest thing I'd seen; my anger at him mixed with compassion for her. That evening, I threw his things out of her apartment and into the trash. I held her as she cried, feeling our story shift. Seeing her pain, I realized our experience had come full circle—she now understood how I felt. I forgave her, my emotions settling at last.

Exes' Responses After Coming Out Trans and Gay

I will set the scene for you. I have always been a person who has been transparent. I have dated people of many genders, many orientations. This has not been a secret to anyone I have dated. There is an interesting intersectionality of reactions when this kind of transition occurs, and then going back to dating men after dating women for a while.

I have had four huge relationships in my life. I dated a straight man in college, which was not healthy. That did not work out; it was very abusive, and we no longer speak and have not spoken in years and will never speak again. That was one that is not related to, but did inform my dating history. That note will go to my first ex-girlfriend, right? I dated her for about 3.5 years. She was a hardcore lesbian; she knew I had dated men and all these things. It did not work out., I don't know, maybe a year or a year and a half break. Then I found my other now ex-girlfriend. We dated for seven years. With both ex-girlfriends, I had told them, "You know, I have dated men in the past, and at some point, I will be transitioning. I do not know when that's going to happen. It took me a long time to start that process. I did not start that process until right before my second ex-girlfriend broke up.

If you can imagine, these two ex-girlfriends have not really been there for the physical transition. They have never seen me with men because I dated them, but they were stuck in this vision of who I was, even though I told them, 'Hey, I have dated men before, and I am going to transition.' I didn't think it would be much of a shock, and I didn't factor in their opinions because they are my exes at this point. When I started transitioning and got back into the dating world, I tried dating another woman for a couple of months, then realized, 'You know what, not for me. I appreciate ladies, just isn't my vibe.'

Once I started really leaning into my transition and taking the testosterone, I became more comfortable in my identity as a gay man. So, I started dating, you know, gay men. Now I am in a significantly committed, loving relationship. I love my partner deeply. So, with that said, before I was in the current relationship, I was still friendly with my ex-girlfriend. By 'friendly,' I mean we would occasionally talk, check in with each other, but not hang out or anything. You know, I had a dog with one of my exes. So, it wasn't as if I really wanted to push her out of my life.

I tried to be diplomatic with them both, but here is the response I received from my first ex-girlfriend when I told her. I recall that on the phone, it was very hurtful. I was on the phone with her. She says, 'Oh my God, I have to say something fast first.' And I am like, 'Okay, go ahead,' and she is like, 'Ew, ew, ew, ew, ew, I can't believe you're dating men.' And I just sat there. I was like, 'Hm, do you think that is okay to say to me?' That is not very friendly or supportive. I realized very quickly after that this was a negative, judgmental energy that needed to leave my life, feeling disappointed but not surprised.

When I told my other ex, who I had been with for seven years, her response was, 'They were both hurtful, but hers was much more hurtful, and she really went after me on the phone. She said, 'I cannot believe you lied to me for all these years.' Have you been gay? You like men? And I was like, look, I told you I dated men well, before we ever dated. Um, but when I was with you, I was with you, you know, I was monogamous. We were together like we were a team. It was just one of those responses that you do not expect from someone who you think has had care for you, and said to me, arriving at where I am comfortable in my identity, and my gender identity and sexuality have nothing to do with you. I was not living a lie. I was very dedicated, but knowing the type of person and their reaction, and all of that, having that negativity just pushed back in your face when you are talking to someone who you think is going to be gentle with your feelings. I did not appreciate it. We no longer speak as well.

It took a long time for me to become who I am proud of, who I am. Anybody who cannot be that for me cannot really call themselves a loyal friend. And so, sometimes people, you just have to go, 'You know what, I thought we could be friendly, and now I can see that we cannot.' I wish you well on your journey.

I know that some people will go to great lengths to keep their exes in their lives. But my exes are exes for a reason. It did not work out. We weren't a fit, like, romantically, and we were not a fit like friendly, but I do appreciate being able to see people for who they truly are and what they truly believe, because at the end of the day, I'm going to be who I truly am and what I truly believe. That's been the experience. I'm not sure if anyone has had that reaction from their exes. If you have had, I feel for you. I try not to think about it too much, but it is part of my story.

Starting Testosterone – Finally Living in and Connecting to My Body

Starting testosterone was the best thing I ever did for myself. For years, I struggled with the fear of losing people if I did what was best for me. Over time, I realized I couldn't keep living a trapped, miserable existence by putting others before my own true, authentic self. When we first got together, I told my then-partner that I would transition, though I wasn't sure when. It took six and a half years into our relationship before I started to make serious moves, because I knew if I didn't, I was going to die.

I ended up losing my partner of over seven years due to my transition and other issues. We went through a lot together, but my transition was too much for her. I moved nearby so we could share our dog, Ducky, and have more space. Discovering her infidelity devastated me. After two months of feeling sorry for myself, I decided to reclaim my life. I weighed over two hundred pounds from stress and unhealthy habits, and resolved to make a real change. My goal: to get fit and prove to myself—and maybe her—what she lost.

My fitness journey began as a form of revenge, but I soon started moving daily—mainly walking in my neighborhood. After losing weight in the first year, I was still too self-conscious to go to the gym, so I bought weights for home and continued to lift for another year. I cut out alcohol and adjusted my diet. By the third year, gaining confidence, I felt ready to try the gym.

I later traded cleaning for a gym membership for about a year. I learned I prefer training alone. I can easily live without the pretentiousness and narcissism of cis-men in the local gym scene.

Navigating The Queer Bar Scene as a Man

I am not a fan of the term "presented as female" before my transition because I never truly identified as female. Let us just say, before I was on HRT, I rarely ever got any attention when I went out from both men and women. I mean, I was not ugly, but I guess I just did not put out a comfortable or inviting vibe because hey, let's face it – I was uncomfortable in my body! That said, I did not expect to receive much attention as a man; the funny thing is, I underestimated myself. I make a way better-looking guy than I did as being perceived as a female. I view this from several perspectives. Having body dysmorphia, it is nice to be appreciated by others and super awkward at the same time.

For thirty-two years of my life, I did everything in my power to avoid mirrors and having my photograph taken. Getting used to my new appearance has come with some new social growing pains that I had not expected. Getting hit on even now is still crazy to me. But I guess, like everyone else, when I was single, I wouldn't always get people hitting on me whom I necessarily had a reciprocal attraction to. The thing is, I never met people with whom I had a mutual attraction at a bar. I seemed to always find myself in the weirdest predicaments at bars with mostly men and sometimes women, too.

I never approach people at bars—I prefer to stay in my spot and see what happens, whether alone or with friends. Going to gay bars as a trans man feels very different now. People approach me, offer drinks, and initiate physical contact—wanted and unwanted. One night in West Hollywood, a seemingly friendly guy struck up a conversation with me and my friend, which led to a very uncomfortable situation.

I could tell he was on Molly, but I did not initially see him as a threat. After living with a couple of addicts, it's not my vibe whether they are friendly or not. It triggers too much shit for me and makes me uncomfortable. At the time, I had not yet mastered the art of displaying disinterest in a casual way when physically approached with unwanted contact. The scenario was either fight or flight. I would either freeze up or get super pissed if someone put their hands on me. Thankfully, writing this now, I have been able to master that; however, that evening, I had not, and things got ugly, but not at first.

I don't remember what my friend and I were talking about, but the guy sitting across from me leaned in and said something that sounded like, "Can I tell you something?" I had a tough time hearing him over the music in the club, so I leaned in and said, "Huh?" Then he put his hand on my face and said, "You've got great skin," and I was instantly creeped out. I mean, it was like a serial killer vibe. I quickly moved back in displeasure. I managed to get out, "No, no man, not cool," and he leaned back in his seat, making a face like he was bummed out. I shot my friend a quick look; he had seen it all go down, and we decided to get up and go stand in front of the bar. I thought that would be the end of that. About five minutes went by, and the same man who was much taller and bigger than me, swooped in front of me as my friend turned towards the bartender.

At this point, I'd had a few beers, and this creep was a total buzzkill. He firmly placed his hands on my shoulders and slid them toward my chest. Common sense should've told him that my first "no" meant "no" in general—as in, "I'm not interested, keep your hands to yourself." He didn't care, and I lost it.

As he moved his big, gross hands toward my chest, the fight in me went from zero to sixty. I wasn't having it. I quickly hooked my right arm under his left, flipping it up and out. As his arm flew, I jerked my arm back, index finger pointed at his face. As this happened, I saw eyes turn toward me. Angrily, I shouted, "I said don't fucking touch me!" His expression shifted to fake innocence – but trust me, he knew. My friend heard me, looked back from the bar, and saw me confronting him. "Come on, Dylan! Let's go!" my friend said, grabbing me as we walked out. He kept me from going to jail because I was ready to knock that guy's teeth in. When a guy puts his hands on me again after I've already warned him, it triggers my C-PTSD from my Mr. Wonderful. The flip side is when it happens with women.

Yes, women have acted this way with me, too. I react very differently; I always freeze up. It's the same reaction I had when my ex-girlfriend would hit me. I could not defend myself because I would never put my hands on a woman. When this happens, I am always shocked because I never see it coming. Frankly, I hold women to a higher standard and assume they will behave with more respect than men, and in my experience, 98% of the time, they do. But then there is that two percent.

One night, I was at the Abbey – the most popular gay bar in Los Angeles - to meet up with a former friend whom I had not seen in about ten years. We had a table outside, and it was the same as it always is. We sat having a fun time, and people would come over and strike up conversations with us and sit down. A taller woman came by and started chatting us up. She seemed cool, so we invited her to sit down. That night, I was specifically in the mood to look at the guys, so much so that I made sure to wear my newest and gayest sweatshirt from my Scruff dating app brand ambassadorship. There was no denying I was signaling for the male gaze as opposed to the female gaze.

A woman and I start hitting it off, in what I have assumed is a friendly way. She is not my type, but she seems nice enough to talk to, and I am a friendly guy, so we keep chatting. As I look off into the bar to get a good scan of the male prospects of the evening, we continue our conversation. We are talking about work, the Abbey, the woman she came there to meet (I, at that point, assume she is a lesbian). Then she compliments me on my deep blue eyes. I thank her, and she asks me how old I am. I say thirty-six, and she cannot believe it, then I feel comfortable disclosing that I am a trans guy. I laugh about how testosterone "keeps me young." This is my go-to response, as it is not the first time this issue has arisen. "Wow, I wouldn't have known." She says with a big smile. At this point, I still do not think anything of it. I think I am making a new platonic acquaintance. Oh, how quickly I would realize my reality and hers were different.

She examined my face after I disclosed my gender identity, then asked about my facial hair. Having had one too many beers, I told her to go ahead and feel it. We continued talking, and when we both mentioned being pansexual, her demeanor turned flirty. She put her arm around me. I froze, uncomfortable and unsure what to do.

I looked back over at my friend, and she was busy talking to her man and caught me mouthing "Help Me" to her out of the corner of her eye. I turn my head back, and the woman kisses me on the cheek, starting to say 'baby this' and 'baby that'. I am terrified at this point because I am not into this chick. I think to myself, "Oh fuck." I froze up again. Luckily, a group of drunk women from a bachelorette party comes over to our table (I know – this is the only time I have been happy to see so many straight women together in a gay bar) and I jump up and offer my seat. I grab my Corona and make my way over to my friend. "Dude. You gotta fucking help me!" I explain what is going on, and then a few minutes later, the woman makes her way back over to our side of the table. My friend and I are standing, and the woman comes over and puts her hands on my face, saying, "baby…" then boom! She lays a kiss right on my lips! I am shocked. "C'mon, baby." She says as she reaches for my hand to try to get me to leave with her. At that point, my friend intervenes, "Oh no, baby's coming with me, he's mine," and my friend grabs my hand and yanks me through the crowd and out onto Robertson Blvd.

"What the fuck was that?!" my friend says, laughing hysterically. "Fuck dude, I don't know! One minute we're talking, the next she's creeping all over me!" I say frustratedly. My friend keeps laughing. "Fuck I don't know what I would've done if you weren't here!" We are both laughing. It's as if I now always have to keep my guard up. Because there have been moments when I have gotten a little too tipsy, not at my sharpest, and then, bam, someone pulls an ambush. It's like, they see their moment of me not paying attention after clearly not having sent any signals that I would be interested, and then they take advantage and lay a big gross kiss right on my lips after I turn my head back in their direction – and stick their tongue in my mouth – ew! This happened to me at Trunks one night after going out alone. I was having a few beers, and this older, unattractive guy pulled this maneuver after I had clearly not sent any signals and was just being friendly and making small talk.

What I have learned is that some people may not be accustomed to people being nice to them, and they may misinterpret it as flirting. When and if I do go out now, it is only with my six-foot-four boyfriend, and I prefer it that way. :)

Chasers and Stalkers

I've had several guys pursue me on multiple platforms, not taking the hint when I'm not interested. Some require a direct message to stop, but I now block people who refuse to respect my boundaries. One persistent guy even escalated from apps to following my Instagram, growing increasingly intrusive despite my lack of response.

Then I noticed he had started to change his profile name; one day it read "Moving to LA," then "Eight Days Until LA," and so on. One day, I get a buzz from him, and his profile name reads "New in Town." Ugh. I hope he doesn't end up being super weird. It turns out that he ends up being creepy AF. I started to get scared and went from posting my Insta Stories in real-time around the neighborhood to only posting videos from inside my house. I had a bad feeling and did not want this man tracking where I would hang out. I became worried because I had posted about my gym at the time, and then had to have an uncomfortable conversation to let them know about this man. I said if anyone came there asking for me, it was probably him, and to please not let him in because I was scared. He then started messaging and tapping me regularly on another dating platform. The scary thing about this other platform was that it would read the distance in feet. One night, I noticed he was close to the grid. It read 1 mile, then moved to 1.2 miles, but later that evening, it read 995 feet and then 661 feet. I felt at that point like I was being hunted. It made me uneasy, then it read 300 feet. I thought to myself, "Is this fucker going up and down my street to see where my place is because he can see me on the grid but not my exact location?" Then it read 200 feet, and I blocked him. I was totally freaked out.

The problem was that he was still following my public Instagram, and with so many followers and having deleted his DMs, I didn't know his screen name or how to block him. So I did what any Internet personality would: I recorded and uploaded a video to my Insta Stories. I explained why I changed my posting and said I was scared because someone was messaging me aggressively across platforms, refusing to take the hint, and I was worried for my safety. Fortunately, that was enough for him to stop. I saw he watched the story and then could block him. Maybe he was harmless and just socially awkward, but I wasn't willing to risk it.

A World Famous Award-winning Adult Performer & I

For the longest time, I wanted to date a trans woman. Back then, I felt that having a relationship with a trans woman could be a good match. I was not having any luck meeting any trans women in real life who were interested in me. So, I did what most single queers in their thirties do – I signed up on a dating app. Ah, yes, dating in the modern age. While the app I signed up for is notorious for NSA, I knew I would have a better chance there, instead of any other platforms, to potentially meet trans women. I created my profile and made sure to list that I was there specifically looking for dates and/or a relationship because I wanted to attract a woman with a similar desire.

Within minutes of posting my profile, I got a message. Expecting another unsolicited pic, I was surprised to see an actual text. The sender was a stunning trans woman. As we chatted, I checked her socials—she was a world-famous, award-winning adult performer. Things just got interesting.

We exchanged compliments and chatted. She was in town for work. Whenever mutual attraction arises on an app, I address the body topic, even with other trans people, due to my lack of top surgery and chest binding. I disclosed, "Hey, just to be upfront, I have not had top surgery. We all have our preferences; I wouldn't be offended if it's a turnoff." She didn't reply right away, so I assumed she was uninterested and left it there. The next day, she messaged me back.

She didn't mind my body, which made me both relieved and excited. When I asked her to meet for a drink, she agreed. She was staying in Burbank; I eagerly planned the trip from Silver Lake. She needed time to get ready, so we agreed to meet later. After another hour, I arrived at the Burbank Holiday Inn.

We planned to meet in the lobby for drinks at a nearby location. Nervous before a date, I headed to the bathroom, then settled into a chair and texted, "Hey! I am sitting in the lobby."

A minute later, she texted that she was just getting into the shower and suggested I Google dinner spots. Her formal tone made me question if I was speaking to a real person. I started to get suspicious and logged back into the app.

On the app, her profile read "Lost All Chats" and listed her six miles away. I realized I might be getting catfished. I texted, "Hey, this doesn't feel right. I'm gonna bounce," blocked her, and left. Walking away, I received another text from a new number offering to FaceTime. Still suspicious, I blocked that one too and returned home. For about a week, doubt lingered. Eventually, I messaged her main social media account and explained the situation. She replied, "Yup, that was me. I kept trying to reach out to you to let you know I was real. But you just kept blocking me." I felt terrible.

We exchanged brief messages. I apologized, explaining my disbelief, while she shared she took extra time getting ready because first impressions were important to her. I apologized again and asked to take her to dinner next time she was in town. She planned to return to LA before the pandemic but had to cancel. We eventually did meet, and she was lovely.

The Accidental Underwear Model

If you had told me even a few years ago that I would be on a date and someone would ask me about being a guy and modeling underwear on the Internet, I would have thought you were crazy! However, this was now my reality – the irony of it all is not lost on me. Having avoided having my photo taken any chance I could get for most of my life and even avoiding using mirrors because I hated how I looked, I knew I was going to have some getting used to transitioning.

To help myself adjust, I started an Instagram account as a form of therapy. Modeling underwear wasn't the plan—I just hoped to grow more comfortable in my body, not realizing how much progress I'd make.

My background is marketing and PR, so I began using Instagram to connect with other trans and queer people online. As an introvert, I found online groups easier to join than finding a community in person. Applying my skills to networking, I quickly found my online tribe.

As I became more comfortable with my look, I thought, 'Let me try to reach out to a few companies to see if I can build a personal brand.' It started working, and with companies that I loved, such as those offering products like dating apps, supplements, clothes, weed, and alcohol, it was wild. Then one day, I went to a job interview at a gay underwear company. In the interview, I was told I was overqualified for the job, which is always with a significant and growing online audience. Their head of marketing did not think to consider establishing a relationship with me for product placement. I thought that was just silly. So, you know what I did? I reached out to another underwear company.

The next week, I introduced myself, and they sent over some products. It was my first underwear shoot. Months later, through another brand relationship, I was offered a strategic partnership with another luxury men's underwear line. They even shared my images on their social media and posted them on their website. It is funny how life works, isn't it? The fact that I have gotten to model men's luxury underwear as a trans man was empowering, and also, having worked hard to lose over forty pounds, I believe you can overcome anything if you are determined enough.

Sex. Work.

Blazing trails is never easy. Coming out as trans publicly was personally rewarding, but professionally, it damaged my earning power. Once, I earned well; after becoming a trans public figure, I could rarely get work outside of sex-related products or services.

It is appalling that, despite so many cisgender people fetishizing transgender people, we still face discrimination in employment. As a transgender man, I have seen that many people seek intimacy with trans people but discard us afterward, or, when they do employ us, treat it as a token gesture without actually viewing or rewarding us as equals. I often say trans people have to work ten times as hard to be taken seriously. We are not given the same consideration as our cisgender counterparts, who are often the ones making hiring decisions, and when we are hired, it feels as if we are valued ten times less.

At 36, I'd reached the top of two careers. Before transitioning, I served as an Associate Creative Director at North America's largest motion picture lighting manufacturer and later as a Creative Strategist at a major rental provider, overseeing creative and marketing efforts for eleven locations. Later, I was subcontracted to manage social media for music legacy accounts reaching millions, yet faced unprofessional comments from management. In the interview, I had clearly stated I was a queer transgender man seeking a diverse, culturally competent team.

Though pleased to be hired, I was insulted by the compensation—twenty thousand less than my previous corporate salary. Opportunities after transition became scarce, so I accepted, hoping for future negotiation. The office culture was inconsistent with the company's self-image, and when people ask why I left, my answer is simple: being trans still means getting the short end of the stick, even when hired.

Months went by with no significant work. I began to explore less "traditional" income streams. Seeking jobs while being a man of trans experience, I learned that trans discrimination is very real. Feeling like a sex object does not align with my career goals. Still, when push comes to shove, people must do what they have to. I have no judgment. Sex sells.

Disclosure vs. Dysphoria

I'm now at a place in my life where I'm able to own the body that I'm in and am not ashamed of it. That said, when I was single and dating as a trans person, disclosure was always part of the process. I know I am not everyone's flavor, and I am okay with that. We all have preferences; I know I have mine, and that is okay.

For myself, I made it a point to refer to the fact that I am trans in many areas of my past dating profiles. Still, even after doing that, there were several times when people messaged me. I could tell they just glanced at my photo and didn't read much about me. Because of this, I also would disclose again over messaging after a conversation had started—typically confirming with something like, "Just to make sure, you did read in my profile that I'm trans, right?" The exchange is normally followed by either a "yes"—they read it, or a "no"—they did not. Some people are cool with it, some aren't, and some would be open to just being friends. Regardless of the response, to lighten the mood, I would always say something like, "Yeah, I'm not trying to surprise anyone."

From my experience, openly disclosing early on via a dating app has been the safest. Early on, before my top surgery, I was transparent about the fact that at that point, I still was binding my chest with no intention of having bottom surgery, and I was comfortable in my body. I liked to be proactive in getting these two things out of the way early on because I wasn't trying to be with anyone who wasn't down with me or wasting my time, you know? I liked to disclose, and I also liked to let my prospective partners know that I was also not dysphoric.

Gay Dating App Brand Ambassadorship Success Story

Let's talk about brand deals and brand ambassadorships. Back in the day, when I had my Instagram account, I would pitch myself to brands. It all started with, 'Hey, I'm doing this professionally for other people, and I'm trying to get comfortable with my body image and all that.' Let me see if I can do that, right? So, it started out as a test.

I sent an email out to Scruff. That was my favorite partnership. Just FYI—I really enjoyed that time, and it lasted about a year. So, I sent them a general email. I was like, Hey, would you ever consider having a trans guy as an ambassador? Five minutes later, I got a yes. They asked for my address so they could send me swag a few times a year, and they would also share some of my posts on their social media platforms. That was great for me: it helped me build my portfolio and my confidence in my body. And what it did, too, was motivate me in other ways, because as a gay trans man, my dating pool was smaller, and I am also extremely selective. So, I wanted to make sure I got out in front of a lot of people. The app helped boost my image, and eventually it led to love for me. So, it was successful in that way! I really enjoyed it. I believe I was the first trans ambassador they had—although I could be wrong, I think I was.

Pretty Privilege After Transitioning

I started my physical transition at thirty-two. I am now forty-one years old. My background includes being a former micro-influencer and working in the adult entertainment industry. I have been featured in Vice and Rolling Stone. Before transitioning, I was a very introverted person—a people pleaser, not confident in my looks at all. What I needed was this transition to feel good and to gain that confidence. I am happy with where I am at physically. However, it has not been easy to get here. I have not been handed anything. At every opportunity, whether it was modeling, press, or any business-related activity, I had to put myself out there. It is often assumed that if someone sees you at this part of your journey, they say, 'Oh, it's so easy for you,' or 'Oh, you were just handed that,' and they discount all of it. The term I would use is "a twenty-year overnight success." And I'm not even in that position, but people don't see all the years, the agony, and the hard work that led to this.

I saw another creator do a video on pretty privilege. I never experienced that before transitioning. I never got a lot of attention, but now I work to minimize it. So, like my old accounts and things I have since cleaned up because of how I wanted to make my transition, I told myself I wanted to get comfortable. If I am going to do this, I'm going to do it full force. And that is why I started posting on Instagram years ago, and I ended up doing all the modeling, because it was therapy for me to get to that point.

And what has come out of this, and my newfound confidence in my-self, has been a couple of things. The people who knew me before my transition started to say things to me like, Oh, you are so conceited or, Oh, you seem like you're so full of yourself now. And I had to explain to them, this is me being confident. I do not think I am better than any-one else. I've never felt this good about myself before, and I should be able to be happy about that. I should also be able to pursue anything I choose because I feel good about myself. And that is what I want to do. So, I have lost some people in that way because there have been some assumptions, and then it is also different meeting new people and them not seeing all the work that was put in before getting to a certain point. And then, just assuming, 'Oh, you just got this deal because you are just this person.'

What I have learned is that I am a mirror and a trigger. For almost every person I meet who is insecure on some level, my confi-dence—whether in taking on difficult challenges, in my body, or in speaking about my identity or sexuality—rattles their cages, though it is not intentional. I am just being my authentic self. When you shine your light bright, there are always people who want to dim it. So, I have learned that I must move through the world differently.

The video I watched was interesting. She said if you're not used to pretty privilege, you have to toughen up and be a bit of a bitch. I agree with that now. I can be nice, respectful, and helpful to anyone. But if people are jealous or insecure—usually because I'm comfortable in my body—they are not kind. Since physically transitioning, I've dealt with a lot of unkind people, both cis and trans, which is unfortunate. But I always say, "hurt people, hurt people."

I wish everybody happiness and good things. But I have had to be a little bit more in my bitch era. I am getting more okay with that. The past year has been particularly challenging for me. But that's the thing:

we should know not to judge a book by its cover. You have no idea what I went through to get to this point. For three decades before transitioning, it was incredibly challenging just to live. We do not know what someone is holding onto inside. If someone is a little bit of light in the world, being happy, I just like to be happy for them, because I know how tough it has been for me.

So, I do believe pretty privilege is a real thing. What comes with it is not always good intentions or motives from the other people. I've had people be nice to me only because of how I look, as they wanted to be with me or get something out of me that would introduce them to something, and to only be nice to people because of how they look, I feel, is the shallowest thing in the world. And it is interesting because some people think of transitioning as a very vain thing. And it wasn't for me; it was about being able to match how I felt about being a good person and how I felt about feeling good in my body. It wasn't about trying to be the hottest, best-looking, or most popular, because I never will be. I never was, I never will be, and I do not want that.

But I do acknowledge that pretty privilege is real. It's unfortunate. I have some pinned pictures in my post of things I've done. I can say I've received hate for everything I've done professionally, whether in public or private. People don't know I deal with haters constantly. I'm half in, half out about putting myself fully online, because I know when I do, it always hits, and what comes with success is a lot of haters.

I think after listening to the Britney book, I kind of want to let it all out, and pretty privilege is a real thing. Being a mirror is tough. At the end of the day, we are all human. We have a story. I am the first person who, if someone wanted to know how I did what I did because they want to do some of it too, and they approached me in a nice way, I'd be the first person to give them advice. However, I have never been approached in that manner. I have been approached quite negatively by both cis and trans people. So, we will see how much I put myself out there. But when I do, I am always successful, and that is something I am proud of. It is nice to take pride in myself. And I hope that most people can take pride in themselves at some point in their lives too.

Years of Binding: What It Did to My Body & How It Physically Limited Me for Years

No one starts binding and imagines twelve to fourteen years later they'll still be doing it. At least, no one I know. I never thought I'd be doing it this long. A combination of financial irresponsibility in my twenties, economic setbacks, and poor credit has led me to many years of binding. What I had noticed from binding tightly for so long: my shoulders have pushed and set themselves forward. Now, they unnaturally sit farther forward than they are meant to. When I take off my binder and try to adjust my shoulders back to proper alignment, I have to push through body memory, and it's uncomfortable. They do not naturally stay in the correct position, which also affects my posture.

As for my posture and back, I developed a slight unnatural curve in my back. This is painful when I try to lie flat on my back. I can feel that the middle of my spine feels slightly weakened, and while it's hard to describe, sometimes it feels like it's floating rather than being steady where it should be in place. It's just a weird feeling. When I stand in front of a mirror unbound and try to straighten my posture, I can see how far my body has grown accustomed to leaning forward. This makes me appear shorter than I am, and when I try to push through my body memory to straighten my posture, it hurts, and I cannot hold that position for a long period.

As for my lungs, here's what I have noticed. When I was thirty-seven, my lung capacity had declined significantly. I now become winded much faster when I train. Before my surgery, when I worked out on camera, I wore a binder—both when weight training and spinning—and had to limit filming my workouts. The binding was tight, with a full trunk tank, which limited my mobility. Taking deep breaths took much more concentration. Over time, I unknowingly began breathing more shallowly. When I trained with the binder, it caused me to take more rapid breaths, making me more prone to shortness of breath and shorter workouts. I stopped training with my trainer (over Zoom during the pandemic) so I could work out independently. Now that I've had my top surgery and am over two and a half years healed, I have no excuses for not working out. Thankfully, I now do it without the binder.

Unwelcome Attention from Cis Het Women & Disrespectful Treatment of My Relationship by Cis Het Women

Triggered by a creepy TikTok comment from a woman, I want to address the unwelcome attention and disrespect from cisgender women I've experienced since transitioning, which I never encountered during my heterosexual relationships. Unwelcome attention has taken many forms for me, both sexual and otherwise, throughout my life.

Public focus is often on men giving unwelcome attention—and understandably so—but women do it too. Since transitioning and gaining confidence in my appearance, I receive more attention. I wish I could feel good without the attention. The only person I want to give attention to is my boyfriend, but that's not my reality.

I try to be respectful, but that's rarely returned. Being treated like an object is awful, and some women are surprisingly forward. I now avoid bars alone, even gay bars, after a woman kissed me without consent. It made me realize that being friendly is easily misconstrued, which makes socializing difficult.

What I've learned in this transition is that I prefer to keep to myself. Many people have not had kind experiences with others, so they tend to read into things or feel comfortable making jokes. I'm not that guy. I don't like that. Many of my partner's female friends haven't seen him date anyone in quite a long time. So, when they meet me, I've heard some things like, Oh, I can grope him because I've known him for twenty years". Ew. And oh," Do you love him? Do you really love him?" Yeah. I do. Would you ask that to me pre-transition and I was with a man? I don't think you'd ask a straight person, do you really love him? Or how about "you all are just dating each other, right?" That was another question. You wouldn't have asked that if I were a straight woman and he was a straight man.

Because we're gay, straight women sexualize us and think it's OK, and it's just creepy. Trying to touch my boyfriend in front of me to get a rise out of me or call him daddy or whatever - that's not acceptable. It's not acceptable because it's disrespectful to our relationship. Again, straight women, you wouldn't do that if it were pre-transition, and I was a straight woman and he was a straight man, you wouldn't be all up on him. It's because you think that because we're gay, you can get away with these jokes and cross boundaries, and it's not acceptable or classy in the least.

I'm here to be myself, not to exchange sexual jokes with strangers. My past required self-sexualization for work, but that's not who I am now. Unwanted sexualized comments—online or in person—are unwelcome and show a lack of understanding of boundaries.

Because someone is trans or gay and you're not, does not mean you can sexualize us; it doesn't mean that you can make jokes and say whatever you want. It is sad because I am a trans man. I used to always feel like, Oh, I can be safe with women. I don't feel like I can trust or be safe with anyone other than my boyfriend. And look, I'm not saying this with some huge inflated ego. I don't think I look spectacular. I don't.

It's literally what has happened in my life, where it's like, I can't go out to places without someone trying to sexualize something or make unwanted physical contact with me or creep around my stuff online and just being fucking weird.

Yeah, ladies, sometimes you think you're being funny and you're really not, and that's not being an ally, and men will forever scare me with that shit, but cis women and men, because you have a friend and they're dating someone new, you should really want to be putting your best foot forward and be respectful. In terms of myself, I just haven't experienced a lot of respectfulness towards my relationship. I would just prefer people to just stop being weird.

Vanity is Boring

One of the most common things people want to discuss with me is my appearance. One of the most frustrating things is when I post a video, and rather than people commenting on the content of the video or the topic I'm discussing, it's about my appearance. I'm quite secure in my appearance. I like how I look. I actually don't need to focus on it, but many people online comment on others' appearances, and I just think that's the shallowest, most boring topic when all people want to talk to me about is looks or how people look, or whatever. That's something that instantly puts me off because it's boring to me.

If we're talking about like, oh, this is how you style your hair, or oh, this is how you style your beard, or an outfit for sure, but if you're making comments specifically on people's appearance, that just shows me how shallow of an individual you are, and you can't connect with people on a deeper level. I think it's so funny because people tell on themselves in conversations too. You're dating people, and someone says, 'Oh, well, I don't know.' What's your original type of person? You go for this or that, and it's like you can tell right then and there that they are a person who's very hung up on looks and extremely leaning towards a narcissistic personality type, because you can tell right there that they're the type of person who dates for looks. And I'm the type of person when I hear that, I'm like, I don't want to socialize with this person because if they're basing one of the biggest impactful decisions of their life, choosing a partner based on looks - looks come and go.

Have we not thought about it? Think about it just in terms of a vehicle, right? You get a car, it's brand new, it's shiny, whatever, it's going to depreciate over time. Yes, you're going to put as much maintenance as you can into that vehicle. Your body is a vehicle. Your face is a, it's the same thing over time. It will depreciate. So if you're dating for looks that says a lot about your personality or if you're talking to people and assuming that everyone is dating for looks that says so much about you because when people say that to me, I'm like none of anyone I've dated has ever looked the same, all different genders, all different races, presentations, everything because I don't date for looks. I date for the quality and content of someone's character, and that's how I view the world in general.

I'm on TikTok, and I will engage with and watch videos that interest me, based on the content of the actual character or topic of the video, not the figurehead in the video. So, it's just really superficial, the comments I get sometimes, or in real life, the way people assume I conduct my life because of how I look. I transitioned because I wanted to feel centered in my body. I feel centered in my body. But I don't obsess about what I look like. I feel sorry for people who come online and have to project those things onto others within their comments, because ultimately, what would be the best use of their time is to sit and self-reflect if they're so hung up on other people's looks. Why are they not focused on their own lives and creating their own content and topics that go deeper than just a surface-level appearance, trying to connect with people on an intellectual level? They don't ever assume that you want to because a lot of people want to sexualize you or fetishize you as a trans person because you changed your look. So, it is quite disappointing when all people ever want to focus on is how you look, and you're like, 'Yeah, I can see in the mirror; I take pictures of myself.'

I am very well aware of how I look, and if you want to give me a compliment on that, it just doesn't resonate with me as much as a compliment or commentary on the actual content of the video I put out or the topics I speak on. Because what do I give a shit that someone thinks my eyes look nice? I don't. What do I give a shit that someone thinks I'm handsome? I don't. I don't care because I'm not trying to get with you. I know how I look. I know how I sound and that there's so much more to our lives than our appearance. Our appearance does play a role in our happiness on some level; it has played one in mine, but it's not the focal point of my journey or my purpose on this earth.

Hawaii Trip and Walking Around Shirtless

It's mid-February 2024, and my boyfriend and I have just returned from Hawaii. The best work/anniversary trip ever! My boyfriend had to work, and then I came out and we celebrated our anniversary. It was a lot of fun! We were there last year, too. Being a trans guy, it was so nice to be outside walking around without my shirt on. Last time I was there, I laid out on the beach without wearing a shirt, but I didn't walk around shirtless.

On this trip, I had finally reached the point where I could feel confident walking around shirtless at this time of day, so it was cool. It felt just as I had always wanted to feel. We had a lot of fun in Hawaii; it was super cool. The people were nice and friendly, and the scenery was just amazing. I didn't want to come back!

Gay Slur

In 2024, my boyfriend and I were walking down the street holding hands as we do. An oversized pickup truck drove by us and shouted the f-slur at us. Now, let me just say, it was giving such big closeted energy because it was coming from the passenger princess side. They were so excited that they saw two gay men that they had to take the most cowardly route to shout at us as they drove past, and the thing about the two of us is that they wouldn't have said it in front of us.

They did, like cowards, because they drove away. Now, my man is a tall, solid guy, standing at six feet four, and I guarantee they wouldn't have said it to his face. When something like that happens, everybody reacts differently, like some people can go, Yeah, that has nothing to do with me and move on with their night. My boyfriend is very mentally tough in that way. But I'm wired differently. What it does is bring up past traumas for me, and that's part of what I'm writing about in my book, and it's kind of like the hurdles I am going through while writing this. There are some parts that are difficult, and some things make me think of other things that happened to me, and that's the third time this has happened to me.

I've had it happen where it was, with a friend, and the same "f" slur was shouted at us, and this was before my transition. I just looked at my friend and said, "Well, apparently, you're gay," and he goes, "Well, apparently, you're a guy". We both laughed it off. The other time was before my transition, when I was dating a woman and we were outside of her work, someone yelled and called us the "d" slur and threw eggs at us as they drove off like the cowards that they are - this isn't new to me. Hate. Violence. Ignorance. Cowardness.

You see, I also guarantee you that the people in that vehicle were clearly triggered, and most of the time when that happens, it's because they're closeted. So, we'll see in a few years when they're released. Just because you live in a big city that calls itself progressive, doesn't mean that these things don't happen. I mean, of course, it's gonna be an oversized truck vehicle. My boyfriend and I have a term for it every time someone's in one of those vehicles and they act a fool; we call it LDE. Now you're familiar with BDE, but we call that LDE. So, I'm sure you can pick up on what I'm putting down. I just wish those people the day that they deserve because life will catch up with them. Karma always does.

Personal Development

How did I get here? The end of people-pleasing brought me to boundaries—seeing both respect and narcissism in action. Setting boundaries has elicited mixed reactions: some are understanding, while others have responded aggressively, unable to see that my goals are not centered on free work or small talk. As a trans person, I have always worked harder for everything, including my body, hustling to create my opportunities. Sharing my life openly has resulted in many questions, comments, and requests—far more often than genuine offers to help. Now, protecting my mental, physical, and spiritual energy is my top priority. I only have so much to give, personally and professionally; my self-care comes first. For those struggling to set boundaries, remember: you come first. You cannot create or grow if you're constantly depleted. Don't feel bad about saying no. I stay well by focusing on fitness, mindfulness, and my own projects—which means turning down requests that drain me. If anyone interferes with my success in these areas, I disengage. That's an act of self-love.

Overcoming Adversity and the Power of Self-Love

The second I started believing in myself, my entire world changed. Fuck what you've been told. You should "do this, you should do that" type of bullshit. All of it. Fuck it. All you have to do is believe in yourself. That's the damn secret. No matter where you're at. No matter what you want. The power you have and need is within you. No one knows you as you know yourself. Your mind can be your greatest ally or your greatest adversary. Train it accordingly. I'm living proof.

I am a badass, and it all comes down to one thing. The secret is I stopped hating myself. I stopped focusing on the "flaws" I thought I had. I let myself breathe, cry, and eventually step into my power. I allowed my mind to visualize myself already living my dream. Every day, I started talking to myself like the badass boss that I am. And now here I am. I made it out of depression, didn't kill myself, am no longer suicidal, survived, and will no longer tolerate any violent relationships. I lost a significant amount of weight and am sharing my story with the world, knowing I've still got more to work on, loving and embracing my imperfections. My story is wild. It all happened, and I'm stronger because of it. I am stronger than most people I know or will ever be, for that matter.

EMPLOYMENT

Diversity Hire

The biggest red flag in a recent job interview was a company's emphasis on how good its people were, to the point where it even made it its tagline. Throughout the interview, they focused more on this than on my actual qualifications, signaling I might be a diversity hire.

If you have to proclaim it, you're probably not living it. On my resume, I list queer organizations to ensure I enter a safe workplace, but I don't want to be pitched on diversity during an interview. It feels like overcompensation for a lack of genuine DEI. To be honest, if you had to say it, you're probably not really going to be it, but I did not know this, and it was very indicative of the overall short-lived experience.

Nonprofit Efficacy & Quality of Services Provided vs. Quantity & Statistics for Funding, My Experience as a Trans Job Seeker

When discussing nonprofits, it's critical to evaluate the quality of their services compared to the quantity of outputs reported for grants and donors. From my perspective as a trans job seeker, I've noticed that some organizations focused on helping people like me fall short when staff do not fully understand my background or needs. This makes it difficult for them to effectively connect me with appropriate opportunities, especially regarding my salary requirements and professional experience.

Although nonprofits receive grants and funding, I question whether the community truly benefits in practice. My own experience began with applying for a staff position at a nonprofit serving the trans community. Despite my motivation to support our community, I was passed over for the job and instead offered their typical client services. During the intake, I quickly recognized a lack of confidence and understanding on the part of the interviewer. In the past, this had led to being offered positions far below my qualifications and needs, which I hoped to avoid this time.

I go through, and they do the interview. He asked me about all my qualifications, trying to understand because I have a vast skill set. But what I'm looking for specifically is a position in brand management, right? I've been doing this for over fifteen years. I have a diverse skill set, a tough job market, and on top of being trans and gay. It's just, that's, that's why I'm there. So, I'm thinking, ' Okay, he's getting it; whatever it's saying, he's going to send me jobs. ' How do you like to communicate? What's best for you? I say email. So, then I get sent Google Chat messages, and I'm like, Why would I download a chat? That's just going to send me an email about the chat. So, you're creating multiple emails. This is not efficient. I'm thinking, ' Alright, this isn't starting out well.

' I give myself a beat, an email comes in at like four forty am with a job that he sends to me that I don't have a background for. I'm not a product designer.

He chose it only because it was tech-related, and we had discussed marketing and salary ranges. Now, they're creating multiple emails for me and sending jobs I'm not qualified for, nor do I want. How does this help me?

In the interview, I want to be completely honest: if I'm applying to a trans organization and the interviewer makes it a point to state that they are cis and not trans, I find myself questioning the organization's decisions as a whole. I don't want to criticize anyone because I genuinely hope these organizations succeed; however, I am not willing to be a test case while they work things out—it's frustrating.

So, I sent an email that morning. I said, Hey, thank you so much for your efforts. You know, I thought we had discussed email for communication purposes and tracking an organization that we would just use email. With that said, I was surprised to get a chat invite. I can see there's no clear understanding of my professional background. I don't have a background in product design yet, but I was provided with that position posting as a follow-up to our intake. For that reason, I find it best not to continue. Wishing you all the best. Thank you for your efforts and your time.

I realize this perspective might sound harsh, but I'm sharing my honest experience with well-intentioned people who haven't been effective. I'm frustrated by this inefficiency—if this is what our trans nonprofits offer, we face serious challenges. For this reason, I consistently support mutual aid over nonprofits, because word of mouth and community support are what truly make a difference in times of need.

Based on my experience, many nonprofits collect intake data for funding purposes but fail to meet the actual needs of trans clients. If they cannot provide the specialized support required, they should not claim to serve everyone. It's especially disappointing when trans-focused organizations fall short, as I genuinely want them to succeed for the benefit of the community.

However, I know I don't have time to be wasting on things where people are learning their processes and there's no confidence backing up the services they're providing. I was told by someone that, personality-wise, I am very particular. I don't disagree. When it comes down to your livelihood, you have to be. If you are walking into a nonprofit that's supposed to help people access networking or the right job opportunities to get aligned with, you have a huge responsibility. You should also be very particular because your work is a direct reflection of you and can affect someone's future who belongs to a marginalized identity.

I've just always felt that way, and sometimes I wish I were less aware because maybe I'd be happier. But I'm not, and those feelings return. Am I always going to feel like a lone wolf in the trans community? Maybe. Maybe not. What I do know is that I have to make things happen for myself. I tried working with nonprofits and have seen what's available—but I'm not impressed. I'm not here to criticize these organizations since they do help so many people find placements that fit their needs. They're just not the right fit for me, and that's frustrating. I realize this may sound arrogant, but if you were in my position, how would you feel?

Being Socialized as Female for Thirty-Two Years and Men's Bathroom Social Mistake After Transitioning

When you're socialized as perceived as female for most of your life, there are certain things you can no longer do after transitioning. I didn't start transitioning until I was thirty-two. Any time I went into the women's room before transitioning, if there was someone in there, there was always a smile or a hi or anything, it was a non-issue because the ladies' room was always just like, oh, I can see that you're there in acknowledgment or whatever, and then go about your business. It's not a thing. It's never been an issue for me. And that's just how I thought everyone was, because again, thirty-two years of my life, that was my experience.

Now, there's no textbook for transitioning and social dynamics. Oh, but if there was, we'd have avoided this one. Let me set the stage. Yes. For all of my life before transitioning, I have entered restrooms, and anytime anyone made eye contact or said anything to me, I would smile, I would acknowledge, and go on about my business. As a man in the men's room, you cannot do that. Here's what happened, and I didn't realize until years later. I was subcontracted by an agency. There was one bathroom on the office floor. The men's room had one stall and one urinal. The sink was over in the corner. I go to the bathroom one day. I walk in, and there is one of the talent managers at the urinal as I walk in, and he hadn't been in the office for a few days. He's at the urinal, and he turns his head, making eye contact with me. And so, for thirty-two years of my life before, when anyone would do that in the bathroom, I'd be like, Oh, hi and go on about my business because I'm literally there to do my business. And that's my only intention.

He makes eye contact with me. I haven't seen him in a couple of days, so I'm just my naturally friendly self, and I go, Oh, hi and he at once shoots his head back and looks down, and I'm like, Hm, that's weird. I go, and I walk into the stall, close and lock the door, and sit down because I have to pee. You know what I mean? For instance, I'm not hiding that I go back into the office, and a couple of days pass, so I ask my client, who I'm subcontracting for, ' Hey, I'm waiting on this email. ' I haven't heard back from him and am met with the nastiest response. She says, "You never speak to him again. If anything, you go through me for him," and I was just like, "Okay, I couldn't understand it at the time."

Like, okay, did I do something because I didn't know? Apparently, he thought I made a pass at him. And that right there is the BIG problem in this world that so many people, specifically cis straight men, think other people's intentions are sexual.

I was literally in a bathroom to use the bathroom. And the sad thing is that I didn't realize this until I thought about it years later. I had a conversation with this guy I was on a date with because he said, 'Oh, I went into the bathroom and some guy said hi to me, and he proceeded to tell me he wasn't good with that.' After hearing that, I just thought to myself, 'Oh, we don't do that as guys, I guess that wasn't great.' I didn't know I was just being myself.

Yes, I didn't realize until years later why I got the reaction that I did, because my intention was literally just to say, 'Oh, there you are,' and then go on about my business, and I was just being polite, like I had been in women's restrooms for my entire life.

Now, what I do is in the bathroom. If I have to go, I don't like using public restrooms, office restrooms, or basically any restroom other than my own. But if I have to, I walk into the bathroom, eyes on the floor and looking at no one, and that is how you navigate the men's restroom. Eyes on the floor, look at no one, nothing. And then the asshole in me is like, oh, that motherfucker thought I was into him?! Wow. What an ego. It really surprises me that people ever think I'm interested or that they would even have a chance, because, to be honest, it's not likely. I don't have an interest in straight men, nor do I have an interest in most gay men either. No, I don't have an interest in my coworkers, and no, I would never put any sort of professional dynamic in jeopardy or purposely go out of my way to make anyone uncomfortable, because that's not who I am. But I can understand now why he thought that. And so, a learning lesson for us all.

Employment Discrimination

From my experience as a transgender man, I believe many employers want recognition for having diverse hires, but still do not treat us as equals, nor do they compensate or promote us at the same level as cisgender colleagues. I often tell people that trans individuals must work much harder just to be taken seriously, yet we are often undervalued compared to our cisgender counterparts, who are typically the ones making hiring decisions. When we are hired, it feels as though we are valued less than non-transgender people.

I read that most people have three careers in their lifetime. By thirty-six, I had already reached the top of two fields. Before transitioning, I was recruited from my role as Associate Creative Director at North America's largest motion picture lighting manufacturer to Creative Strategist at the world's largest lighting and grip provider, overseeing creative and marketing operations across eleven locations. I'm a highly intelligent, dedicated worker.

Three years and nine months into my transition, I was subcontracted by a boutique agency to manage social media for world-famous music legacy accounts. My work reached millions daily. Despite this, I experienced unprofessional, ignorant, and homophobic comments from management. During the interview, I disclosed that I am a queer, transgender man seeking a diverse and culturally competent environment, and I was pleased to be offered the job. However, I found the compensation insulting given my background. I took the position in 2019 at a salary of $20,000 less than my 2014 corporate role.

After my transition, opportunities in my fields of interest became rare. Despite my dissatisfaction with the low rate, I accepted the position in the hope of renegotiation after a year. I was surprised that the organization's casual humor conflicted with how they promoted their inclusive values during interviews. When people learn about the prestigious accounts I worked on, they always ask why I left. The short answer: as a trans person, I became tired of having to educate colleagues on professional treatment instead of being able to focus on my actual work.

In detail, I had to address why comments about my work and anatomy—made by a heterosexual cisgender woman—were unprofessional and unrelated to the job, serving only to demean me. The final straw came when I learned that upper management referred to all gay professionals using a slur. Disgusted, I quit that afternoon.

HEALTHCARE

Going to the Doctor While Trans

I like my doctor, but each visit follows the same pattern. When I ask a trans-specific question, I'm told there isn't enough data yet. For cis people, imagine every visit about a health concern being met with a similar response. More research is desperately needed on aging and health issues for trans men.

When studies on drugs are done, it's rare to see trans individuals included. If they are, research favors amab people. When I check my testosterone or other issues, I usually get, "We don't have enough data on that yet."

I expected to deal with doctors and surgeons as a trans person—it hasn't always been easy. I often get anxious before appointments, and pharmacy issues, like delays in getting testosterone, have been a hurdle for weeks. I'm currently out of T, but I hope my doctor can resolve this. She's good at her job, but trans-related research, particularly for afab people and aging, is still lacking.

If you've run out of hormones, you know how rough it feels. I trust my doctor to fix it, but medical research for afab trans people isn't where I'd like it. It limits what I can learn about aging as a trans person.

That's why I value older trans people sharing their medical experiences. Their knowledge is invaluable, especially since I'm forty-one, and my experiences can help younger people. Our community is our best data source.

The IUD

Yes, I am a trans guy who hasn't yet had a hysterectomy, that shit's expensive! Like a lot of other trans men, I hadn't been to a proper gynecologist and avoided going. I knew as a dude if I ever got pregnant, I'd be upset. I had to bite the bullet. Thankfully, my doctor was the best possible I could have ever asked for.

We discussed options, and I wanted to double down on my protection and opt for the ultimate choice. So, IUD it was! Now, I didn't research if there would be pain involved with it. Looking back now, that wasn't very bright. Think about it, someone's shoving this contraption into your vagina, through your cervix, and into your uterus, of course, it's going to hurt! At the clinic, my doctor had two IUD options. Since I didn't have insurance, I would have had to pay out of pocket, which would have been either $150 or $ 1,000. Naturally, having always lived on the brink of poverty in Los Angeles and being house-poor as a renter, I opted for the $150 choice. However, my body had a whole other plan; it was not having any of that $150 IUD business.

My doctor tried the $150 IUD, but it was rejected. She used the $1000 one, which fit but caused intense pain and lightheadedness. Kindly, she charged me for the $150 one. The pain worsened on my taxi ride home, every bump aggravating it.

That drive felt endless, with traffic, potholes, and construction making my pain worse. At home, I took Ibuprofen, ordered food, and stayed in for three days. The struggle was real. Years later, replacing the IUD became unbearably painful. I switched to an arm implant, which I'm happy with.

Surgeries I've Had While Transitioning

I'm going to discuss the surgeries I've had and the potential ones I'm considering for the future. A little disclaimer here: this is my experience, which I am open to sharing. Not every trans person is open to sharing these things. It's not proper to just go out and ask someone who's trans about surgeries.

So anyway, the surgery I've had is a top surgery. You could see through some of my online videos that I chose to have the large scar. That was based upon my anatomy, but also on the fact that I want to be visibly trans in a way that I can. That was what was right for me. Having that surgery was very mentally taxing on me. It took me fourteen years to bind to get there; that's what I needed to feel comfortable in my body.

Now, that's not to say I might not want to, you know, freshen things up here and there, but what I needed to feel good about my transition was that I needed top surgery. I'm incredibly proud of myself for making that happen. Things I'm considering for the future include body masculinization, which involves slimming out and squaring up my midsection. It's a little liposuction there, just making things a little less curvy. There's potential for that. That gives me quite a bit of anxiety, and I don't feel like that is a life-or-death situation that I need to happen, so it may or may not happen in my lifetime. If it happens, great. If it doesn't, I'm fine with that too. And that's the same approach with facial masculinization.

I love the fact that I am fortunate enough for my beard to have grown in the way it has, as it helps shape my face. There's a lot that you can do with that, so I'm happy with that. That said, I would be all for the handsome squid ward look. You know, I want to refine it a bit, make the edges a little sharper, but I'm okay if that doesn't happen. Another one. We discuss gender-affirming care, and as it relates to hair, right? So, I'm not opposed because my hairline has been receding since this transition started. I'm not opposed to that happening either, but again, if it does, great. If it doesn't, great. Like, I got a nice-shaped head. I can shave it down if necessary. I'd prefer to have hair, but even if I don't have hair that grows out of my head, I can always put it on, too. So, to me, there's always a workaround, but the one surgery that I needed to be able to wake up and be comfortable in my body, I am fortunate enough to have had.

When meeting new people, some ask deeply personal questions about my body without hesitation. While I choose to share details online where I feel safe, intrusive questions in person feel inappropriate and entitled. I prefer not to be asked unless it's in a medical context.

In real life, I don't want to be asked those questions unless I'm with a medical professional, which is what we're discussing. It's really nobody's business but mine. Today I had someone comment. On what was in my pants online, that's an immediate block. Number 1, why are you thinking about it? Number 2, you have no chance. So, don't think about it. And then I have to think about you thinking about like that, that's fucking weird. Always off limits. Don't ask people what's in their pants, cause it's none of your business.

As I mentioned, these are the surgeries I'm considering for the future. When I think of all the things I've gone through in this transition, the relief I've gotten from that surgery has been lifesaving. It's what I needed to get out of bed in the morning. I wore various binders for over fourteen years. It really affected my health. I really never felt comfortable. It's amazing to simply get up and put on a shirt without feeling like I can't breathe. I feel like I can breathe now, literally, because I can breathe better out of the fucking binder, but like I feel at peace in my body, and that's what surgery has done for me, it's brought me a bunch of peace.

The thought of maybe going under again, it's a lot, and I've been through quite a bit. And sometimes the things I've been through don't really hit me until years or months later, or certain things, so I'm in the process of dealing with it right now. It's hard because things are coming back to me. Sometimes it just takes all my energy out of me, and I don't really know how to convey that other than I don't think my body and my mind are physically up for the challenge of another surgery anytime soon. I am proud of where I'm at, I'm proud of how I've gotten through the tough things, and I know that I can get through more tough things as well. I always tell people, trans people, we are some of the strongest people you'll ever meet because we've had to work extra hard for certain things that people are just born with. So, when I think that way, I'm the master of my own universe; I can make anything happen that I want to, so if I want to, I will.

Top Surgery Journey

I got my entire top surgery covered. This proves the power of persistence—no matter your situation, you can make things happen if you persevere. It took me over fourteen years. Why so long? As someone low-income and pre-transition, my earning power was limited; jobs often paid poorly, and I rarely put myself first, whether financially or socially. I focused on helping partners instead.

Fourteen years of binding took a toll—shoulders pushed, poor posture, and ongoing physical and emotional pain. Work came and went; I'd start jobs, but concerns about transition made me leave. Working for myself brought inconsistent income, and clients would drop me when they learned about my transition. Money was always tight, but I remained determined to make surgery happen.

This is why I tell people: where there's a will, there's a way. Living in California, I was struggling to make ends meet, relying on food stamps, and trying to survive the pandemic. I applied for Medi-Cal through the Department of Social Services. They already had my records, so I pursued a name and gender change. Even legally, I faced ridicule, including from a social worker on the phone. I escalated the issue to the Head of Health Services in Sacramento, who ultimately resolved the matter.

I went to my doctor, and they had to refer me to a surgeon. I was like, 'I want to go to the best surgeon, and he's in San Francisco.' They were like, Why don't you just pick someone in Los Angeles? It will be easier for you. You don't have anyone there. I thought, 'No, I want to go there.' They sent a referral for someone who had like two years of experience outside of medical school in Los Angeles. And I was like, What is this? So, I dealt with the doctor's referral office, and I said, 'No, get a referral for the surgeon in San Francisco.' This is who I want. Then they received the referral, and it was processed. I was like, ok, great. I didn't know how I was going to make it happen because at the time, I had no money. I live in Los Angeles, and I don't know anybody in San Francisco, and I was like, alright, let's try and figure this out.

I was watching TikTok, and I came across a video that introduced me to a nonprofit called Queer Care. And so, through there, I was able to find a place to stay during my surgery. I had very lovely volunteers who would come and check on me, help me take my medicine, and do all these things. It was a huge blessing that I never thought would happen in my life. But you think about it like, all right, how did I get there? Like, how did I get around? I thought, 'Okay, how am I going to get there because I don't have a car?' I don't know anybody. What am I going to do? So, I looked around, and there is another nonprofit called Angel Flight West, which provides medical transportation. If you're having a medical procedure and you're on a low income, you can apply through them to see if they will volunteer to take you to and from your appointment, even if you need to fly. So, I got to fly on a jet out there and fly back on a jet. It was actually one of the biggest accomplishments of my entire life. I surprised myself.

Queer Care reimbursed me for transportation and some food while I was in San Francisco. I got the surgery and surgeon I wanted, thanks to my determination. As Mr. Rogers said, "Look for the helpers." After years of feeling alone, seeking help led to support.

During that time, many things happened. Many people gave up on me, but I never gave up on myself. So, I hope that part of my story may help someone. Additionally, a significant aspect of the story that I also left out is that when you undergo surgery, or at least when I did in the state of California, which is where I live. It's different for everyone else. I needed a letter from a therapist to say, Hey, you're good to get your surgery. I wasn't seeing a therapist, but there is a program called the Gender Affirming Letter Project. There was a lovely therapist who joined me on Zoom. We had a session, and she wrote me a letter, which helped get the process started.

There have been many people along my journey who, despite not knowing me, have helped me. It's something I'll never forget. So when a trans person reaches out to me or when someone says they have a trans family member, I will always take that moment to have that conversation, to listen, to offer advice if people want it, to help because in the moments I need it, people were there for me. I wouldn't be here if it weren't for them. I'm incredibly happy and grateful to have had the opportunity to do this and share this story. It's just one of those things that, if you're going through it, just know that you'll get through it, just keep going.

The Wildly Comedic Reason Why My Top Surgery Almost Didn't Happen

So you just read my crazy story of how my top surgery finally came together after fourteen years - but it almost didn't happen for one very, very stupid reason. Before my surgery, COVID was going around, and we were still very much in the pandemic, and my surgeon's office informed me that I needed to have a PCR test to be allowed into the office and to be cleared for surgery. I needed to have a COVID test, a specific type, a couple of days before the surgery. At the time, there were only a limited number of locations that would do it, and so I saw CVS and thought, 'Okay, cool, I'll book that one.'

At the time, I was living in West Hollywood, but I had to go to the CVS in Hollywood. It was located near Avalon by Capitol Records. I make the appointment, and I show up. I can't get in the front door, so there's a drive-through. Important note: I do not own a car, so I had to walk up through this drive-through with a mask. I'm thirty minutes ahead of my scheduled appointment, and they said, "Oh, you're early, and actually we can't administer any sort of test.. We can't give you the test for you to give back through the box unless you have a vehicle". Wild.

At that point, I'm thinking, I've gone through all this shit, all this struggle to get this surgery, and this is what's going to stop it, oh hell no.

And I said, "Look, I need to get this for my surgery. I don't have a car. I can't afford an Uber. What do you all want me to do here?" And they're like, sorry, sir, that's how it is. So then I started to lay it on, "you can't say that, we've got to figure something out here. I need this. This is for my surgery." And then I'm told," alright, we're not supposed to tell you this, but, if you go get one of those Bryd scooters and come back in a half an hour and wheel it through the drive-through, that's technically considered a vehicle and then we can give it to you and you have to take the test here and then you can drop it right in there" as they pointed down to the drive-through dropbox. Bewildered I asked, "are you joking?", and they said," unfortunately, I'm sorry to say that we're not." So, of course, I was like, OK, let's do this then.

So, I go for a walk, and as I turn the corner, there it is - a Byrd scooter. I drag it, and I sit down on the sidewalk for like twenty-five minutes, and I'm looking at my watch, and I'm like, OK, and I get the scooter and I wheel it through the drive-through. At this point, I have a line of running cars waiting behind me. Directly behind me is an oversized SUV. As I walk back up to the window, holding the scooter handlebars, I say, " I'm back, remember me? Yeah, can't forget, can you?"

So, they give me the test, and it's all locked up with plastic and the little swab and everything. And I am standing in a CVS drive-through, giving myself a COVID test, swabbing my nostrils with all these people behind me, cars running, I remember the overpowering smell of exhaust fumes, all the while I am also trying to balance this Byrd scooter against me so that I can be following the rules so that my test will be processed. So, then I complete the test, it goes through, and I get my results a while later. I was all set to go, but that almost delayed my top surgery. It was the wildest shit ever. Being broke in Los Angeles as a trans person during COVID, during my transition, during all of this, has shown me how tenacious I am. So if you're going through something tough, just don't give up.

Top Surgery Year Two Update

In September of 2022, I had my top surgery. In September of 2024, I like what I see. Nice to wake up in the morning. I struggled for over fourteen years binding my chest. Thirty-two years of my life without pursuing my transition. I'm forty-one now. I struggled in my body. I was at war with myself for my own happiness. I just didn't want to be alive for a large portion of my life because my body wasn't matching up with my mind. I struggled. With suicidal thoughts since the age of six, they stopped when I started to pursue my physical transition. This saved my life. It's nice to wake up in the morning without that dread. It's such a relief to still be here and be in the form that I had always dreamed of.

There were so many times that I could have given up. There were so many times that I wanted to give up. And I'm so glad that I didn't. And if you're in a position in your life where you don't know how to make something happen, but you really want it and it will improve the quality of your life, just hang in there and don't give up. This has massively improved the quality of my life.

I wouldn't give up the struggle because I feel it's made me a much more compassionate human being. I have witnessed the best and the worst of society during this transition, through the pursuit of my own happiness and bodily autonomy. I have seen the best and worst in people. I have learned so much. I have emerged from this so wise and at peace. For thirty-two years of my life, I felt like I was at war with myself because I wasn't aligned and centered in my body where I needed to be. I wake up in the morning now, and I have peace. You spend thirty-two years of your life without feeling peace; it takes a while to understand how to sit with it.

I'm adjusting to what peace feels like because I'm like, well, this is the best it's ever been. It's only going to get better, I tell myself, because it's still an adjustment. To go, OK, in my body, I'm good. This saved my life, this changed my life, and it improved the quality of my life. I had so many people go, "Well, do you really need to do that?" These were people I was close to, with a heavy emphasis on the word "were".

I just wanted to put this out there to say that if someone is willing to share their journey about their body, whether it's related to transitioning, weight loss, health management, or anything else, I'd love to hear it. If someone is willing to share their thoughts and goals, and if they're not going to hurt you, you don't need to pass judgment or question them. You just need to know that the person is on track with what they need for their happiness and to support them. I'm now happy to get up in the morning. It's nice to be able to say that.

Testosterone Eight-Year Check-In

Eight years on testosterone has brought positive and significant changes for me. The decision was right for my transition and has helped me become more comfortable in my body. My fat distribution changed, and I lost weight. Early on, I worked out every day to support these changes, which became more noticeable over time.

Body hair was one of the major changes. It began in an unusual manner and gradually increased over time. Now, I'm quite a hairy man. My voice also got lower. I explored voice classes but decided I was happy with it. The main thing I wanted was a change in appearance to feel more comfortable, and that's what happened. Some changes appeared gradually, and some may never show—there's an element of luck.

My hairline receded considerably over time. I also gained muscle mass from working out—after starting, I could burn calories much faster than before. Now that I've had surgery, I need to return to a regular lifting routine, although I've been cautious about resuming weight lifting.

Testosterone also changed my emotional landscape and social experience. Over time, I became emotionally steadier. Socially, my experience of navigating society as a man has changed—I now find myself less social and outgoing, as people sometimes misinterpret my intentions. While that can be difficult, overall, the changes have been positive for me.

The greatest benefit of being on testosterone is that I care far less—if at all—about other people's negativity. Testosterone has definitely toughened me mentally. Many claim testosterone stops them from crying; I barely cry now myself, although I used to. Cutting toxic people and places from my life was essential during my transition. Taking testosterone was the best decision I've ever made, and I'm committed to it for life. Transitioning is the hardest thing I've faced, but easily the best.

Gynecologist

Yesterday, I went to the gynecologist for a colposcopy. During the examination, my doctor asked if I was experiencing pain, and I was. We discovered my uterus is tilted, which was unsettling since I had never heard of that before. Now, I get to learn about it firsthand (sarcasm).

There's little information about aging as a trans man, which is why I want to share my story. After nearly nine years on testosterone, I am experiencing discomfort and some atrophy. Visiting the gynecologist as a trans man is complex, but regular tests remain essential. Discussions of reproductive rights often lack inclusive language, yet we face many of the same issues cis women do.

LESSONS & ADVICE

Things I've Learned During My Transition

One of the most important lessons I've learned during my transition is the power of not reacting. Sometimes, a nonverbal response is more effective than a verbal one in difficult situations. For example, when people challenge or provoke me because I'm trans, I now focus on staying calm, using silence, or asking them to repeat themselves. This tactic has been helpful both at work and in my social life.

If I ever signed something under pressure, here's why: If you're being harassed at work, don't always run to HR. Instead, document every incident. When you're ready, schedule a meeting and let them know you've kept a record. This approach is more powerful than frequent complaints.

Documenting and remaining calm can help alleviate the anxiety of those who bully or try to exclude you. When others hope to rattle you, composure brings you closer to justice. In social situations, a look or a silent stare often makes people more uncomfortable than their attempts to disturb you. Throughout my transition, I've learned countless lessons. The most important is how to assert myself strategically.

What To Do If You're Not Selected by a Surgery Fund

If you submit to a trans surgery or support fund, and you're not chosen, here's what to do. I want you to learn from my experience and hopefully avoid what I have gone through. I want to make it better for the next round of trans people by just sharing some advice. The reality is that, with these funds, the need, and the time, not everybody can be funded. Not everyone can be helped with these, and if you're rejected, if you don't hear back, or if you just don't achieve your goal when you thought you would, here's what to do.

First thing is that I breathe; it's going to be okay. I applied to so many things and was rejected over and over again. Not being accepted for something from your own community can hit a lot deeper, but the reality is that the demand is very, very high. There are so many people who need what we need. The first thing I told myself was, you know, that sucks, but you have to be happy for the people who received it because it was their time. It may not be your time, but eventually it will be.Secondly, I will repeat this forever - don't give up hope! It is OK. There's a certain criteria for every fund that gives out, and sometimes people are prioritized over others. It couldn't matter how much great volunteer work I could have done. It couldn't matter how much I spoke up in the media. It couldn't matter how many good things I put out into the world. If I'm a former adult business worker (which I am) and I'm up against someone who's a volunteer firefighter, they're going to get it before me. That's just the reality of what part of my story was.

I would apply to these funds and through trans companies that would fund surgeries for other people, and I would see the people that they would help out, and I would get it. I was happy for them, and I still am. Eventually, I did get mine through different routes. So, that's where I come to number three: explore other opportunities, don't give up, and create opportunities for yourself too. There are many charitable organizations that have helped me, not just one.

Check out my website to view organizations that helped me. It took me fourteen years to get my surgery, but when it happened, it was fully covered. I had all my needs taken care of, including food and transportation. If a fund can't help you, know there are other paths to getting support. Keep pushing. My own journey spanned fourteen years—I nearly gave up many times as I watched others achieve my dream. But in time, it was my turn too.

The main takeaway is to avoid bitterness if you don't get the help you need right away. After achieving your goals, remember your own struggles and use that understanding to help others in their journeys. It's essential for us as trans individuals to support, inform, and uplift one another as we strive for greater equity.

Sharing my story helps show others they can overcome challenges without becoming bitter. If you're not selected for a fund, don't give up. Achieving your goals is possible with persistence, and helping others later can make a difference for our community.

Sometimes, the best thing you can do is to just share your story and say this is why, this is why we raise money, this is why we have these organizations, this is why we have these charities, it's because we need them, because we don't want our people to struggle. That's kind of what I think my life's purpose is: I don't want the next trans group of people to struggle. I don't want them to live in poverty. I don't want them to live through the things that I have. I want them to know that, unfortunately, if they do have to experience that, they can, and it will make them stronger. They will be okay as long as they believe in themselves and keep going.

Being Your Own Success Story

Everyone defines success differently. In 2002, I moved to Los Angeles for film school, determined to pursue a career in the industry. I worked in production, pursued different paths, but none of the jobs fulfilled me.

I felt I truly 'made it' after my inward journey and transition—getting surgery because it was essential for my sense of success. For me, being successful means waking up happy to be myself and not feeling hopeless. That was the reality for most of my life before my transition.

Transitioning is my success. When I reach my own success, others may try to humble me, often by referencing my past in the adult industry. Yet, even by fame's standards, I've been featured in Rolling Stone, Vice, and Newsweek, and have worked as a convention model. I know I'm my own success story, regardless of outside measures—as long as I meet my own, I'm satisfied.

Many people struggle to see your success if they have not pursued their own goals. Everyone filters success through a personal lens. Use that to keep your focus: define success for yourself, and if others try to undermine you, remember your achievements are your own.

How I Handle Being Unappreciated

At some point in our lives, we're going to feel unappreciated, right? People are not going to want to recognize our talents; they're not going to appreciate our time and efforts, whether it's work or personal relationships. Now I've come to the point in my life where I'm like, OK, you don't appreciate this. You don't value me. You don't see what I'm bringing to the table, so go out and find something better.

If someone doesn't appreciate me—at work or personally—I let them go find something better. Usually, it's inexperience that keeps people from recognizing value. Most of the time, they come back. Now, when I feel unappreciated, I leave, because I believe in staying where I'm celebrated.

Vision Boards

I've successfully used vision boards to set and achieve goals in the past, and I continue to use them to plan for my future. For example, with my first vision board, I included a celebrity influencer I admired, and later met him in person, just as I'd envisioned.

I also had a cutout of a male chest on my vision board, which I realized in my own life. Seeing these images daily kept me hopeful and focused on my goals, especially during difficult times. I'm grateful for what I've achieved through this process. If you don't have a vision board, consider making one.

Re-Examining My Blueprint of Love

When you notice repeated patterns in your life, you must re-evaluate yourself as the common denominator. In love, people often want to blame others, but this journey is about my self-analysis—understanding how my upbringing (a narcissistic father, an overly giving mother) shaped my views on love and relationships. Ultimately, I broke the cycle.

The common denominator in my personal relationships was me. Now, I ask: Why do I receive the same treatment from people in both my business and personal life? What do I need to do to align positively with myself? What boundaries and changes do I need to attract healthy relationships? We're always a work in progress, and that's a good thing—each day presents an opportunity to improve.

When you go through a transition, everyone around you does too. As you grow and speak your truth, some people may try to gaslight or discredit you because your growth unsettles them. Stay true and get louder—never diminish yourself. Life is constant change: your tribe stays, others teach lessons, and the Universe repeats them until you learn. I finally understood love starts with self-respect, self-love, and self-awareness.

Am Writing (This Book)

Writing my life story means reliving a lot. The more I do this, the less I want to talk. I'm speaking out my book before editing because that's what works for me. As you've seen, my story includes ups, downs, laughter, and drama. Ultimately, it's about perseverance, even when discussing sensitive lows. It's not all been bad. There have all been pretty funny stories in here as well. I'm in the challenging part of it, but I'm proud of myself for being able to speak on it.

Life Lesson While Writing

One of the biggest lessons from this transition is to prioritize my peace. I used to be a people pleaser, always available to support others. But doing so drained my energy. I realized I wasn't focusing on my own happiness in the process.

I realized I needed to prioritize my goals and happiness. As I focused on this, people who were accustomed to my support began to drift away. When people take this change personally, I remind myself that I'm on track, pursuing my own happiness. It wasn't about losing people—it was about gaining myself.

If you ask people about me, you'll hear different opinions. I'm not the most outgoing, social, or friendly person, but I choose happiness on my own terms. I manage my time—and my interactions—deliberately. I view diet not just as food, but as everything I consume: media, energy, environment. If I sense a bad vibe, I simply move on rather than confront it. Not everyone is meant for your journey; this is about maintaining happiness, not dismissing others.

I know how to keep this ship sailing, and that's a big life lesson. There's a quote, sometimes attributed to Tom Hardy: ask anyone about me and you'll hear everything from 'great guy' to 'asshole.' Believe them both—I treat people accordingly. This fits my experience.

My Biggest Life Lesson

My biggest life lesson is to be yourself. Not everyone will accept you, but the right people will. Society often shames authenticity, but embracing it helps you find your people. Many didn't understand my vision for myself, but I believed in it from a young age. Drawing my future self was how I began manifesting who I wanted to become, even before I understood my identity.

Now, I'm the happiest I've ever been because I am authentically myself. Things continue to improve as I embrace who I am. I don't call myself a role model, but you can learn from my example: be yourself, and you will be celebrated for it.

Red Flags When Meeting New People - Creepy Men

Since starting my transition, I've met many creepy cis gay men. If you're meeting me for the first time, please don't assume I want physical contact; I rarely even want to shake hands, and I certainly don't want to hug you if I don't know you well and we are not close. I don't understand who started to push the idea that we need to physically make contact upon meeting and/or leaving a group of people, but it was probably some weird cis man that started that, and then they all just jumped in on it. I'd rather just not. Physical contact from me is reserved for those most meaningful to me and most people. If you have to ask, I probably don't want to. Avoid making sexual jokes or getting too familiar too quickly—those are red flags. Anyone who tries to get close very fast seems toxic or has questionable motives. That's why I keep my guard up.

Having Unsupportive People in Your Life

As a child. I grew up with two brothers, and I was not and am not the favorite. I am a proud black sheep. I'm ok with being the black sheep. But as a little kid, I couldn't understand for so long why my family would play favorites. It just didn't make sense why you watch your siblings get championed for their dreams and their achievements, and you don't, you kind of wonder why, and you build this self-talk, and then you go into your teenage years and you go into your young adult years and you have this self-talk and you go, oh well, why, why? And in your mind, you have this narrative that people just don't want to support me. And so, if you are at that point right now and you feel that way, I hope this helps you.

The best thing I did in my life was to let go of anyone's thoughts or judgments about me. And when I started to do that. That's when I really started to live. I've had jobs. I've lost my job. I've been in a position where I had to make money and went into the adult industry, and that's really where I lost my caring about what anyone thought, because I had to do what I had to do to take care of myself, and I'd do it again.

More people are out there who will just support many that you don't even know yet. So long as you don't listen to that inner voice that was put there by insecure people who are projecting their own nonsense to you. There are supportive people out there. You will have many people who will champion you. They'll be happy about your dreams and your success. If anything, and you see me online, take from it, put yourself out there, you never know what positive can happen.

Transitioning and Jealousy - How I Manage People with Bad Vibes

The most jealousy I've ever dealt with in my life has been during my transition. In two very different ways, and so it's something that I now realize will constantly happen ever since transitioning. This is why and how I deal with it. There are two versions of jealousy that I run into. I used to be really depressed, really sad, not wanting to live, and then when I started to put myself first and I went through my transition and I did all these things and I changed like glow up hello, I have this light inside me, this happiness that it doesn't matter, if you're cis or trans, you can see it because I'm much happier than I ever was.

When I come into contact with people who don't necessarily have that for themselves, it sometimes comes out in jealousy towards me, but often it inspires other people to pursue their dreams. For some people, I really rub them the wrong way if they are lazy and insecure, because my worst enemy is a lazy, jealous person who is bitter about not making things happen for themselves. If they haven't pursued their goals, jealousy often manifests in subtle, passive-aggressive ways, such as occasional, seemingly innocuous comments. When I start to notice that, I begin to distance myself from those people, regardless of who they are. Friends, family, coworkers, acquaintances, whatever. I'm not having that energy around me. I'm just not dealing with it.

The other side of jealousy that I have dealt with, and that I still deal with to this day, unfortunately, is from other trans community members, specifically trans men. It's a disappointment because, personally, I've always wanted to be part of a community of friends who've gone through something similar, so that I could feel like maybe someone could understand me. Unfortunately, what I've experienced is that it tends to go through a phase with certain people, but not with everyone. Obviously, not everybody acts the same, but this is how it's gone down with quite a few trans men for me.

Some trans men are friendly at first, then become negative with backhanded comments. A wise person once said A jealous person is your worst enemy. I block people who tease or bully, since I don't see camaraderie in that. I'd rather connect with those who genuinely support me. Online, some jealous people follow me just to hate, which I don't understand. I don't have many trans friends in real life, but I have acquaintances online and positive experiences overall – except for a small minority.

I've learned to recognize jealous behavior early. After nine years of transition, it's easy to spot. When people try to diminish my happiness, I simply block them. You don't have to tolerate negativity if you glow up or find happiness.

When people are overly friendly right away, I see it as a red flag—often, they turn negative. Some just want to be close for the wrong reasons, which is why I'm cautious about who I let in.

Transitioning and Envy

People will be envious or jealous of you at some point—it's just life. You can't control their feelings. What they often overlook are the daily struggles, hard work, and dedication that underlie your achievements. People often judge based on perceived "overnight success," but in reality, every goal requires relentless effort. When those goals are reached, envy is inevitable.

I remove envious energy from my life quickly because it makes me uncomfortable. If someone can't be happy for others and turns to jealousy instead, they should look inward—other people's achievements aren't threats. It's a personality trait some never unlearn.

During my transition, I put myself first for the first time. This made me realize how people had been treating me all along. Some were fine when I was at a certain place, but now that I've grown, they're uncomfortable. I expected certain people to be happy for me, but they weren't.

Their reactions were about their own feelings, not my achievements. For example, my brothers are both talented musicians, and I'm happy for them. I have other gifts. When I was quoted in Rolling Stone, their reactions reflected these dynamics.

My younger brother authentically celebrated my Rolling Stone article. My older brother, also in the music industry, only acknowledged the article's quality without much excitement. Growing up, I never craved attention and avoided being in the spotlight, unlike my older brother, who thrived in it. Now that I'm living authentically and getting attention, he became envious and distant. That, along with other issues, led to us not speaking.

After transitioning and stepping into my power, people started thinking I was full of myself simply because I was finally happy and authentic. That can trigger envy in those who haven't chased their own goals. If I bring out envy, it's not my problem; it's theirs.

If you notice people acting jealous as you become more confident during your transition, let it go. Don't carry their pain—it's not yours. Celebrate yourself. If someone says they're jealous, remind yourself it's about their work, not yours. One lesson from transitioning is that you may inadvertently trigger those who are unwilling to pursue their own goals. That's their responsibility, not yours.

I genuinely love seeing trans people succeed and cheering others on; those are the people I choose to surround myself with. Supportive people create a positive environment. Focus your energy where you want results. Remember, others won't see your journey, just the outcome. When faced with envy, acknowledge your own hard work and continue moving forward.

Transitioning taught me that seeing someone do what you aspire to can inspire, not breed envy. If someone else can do it, you can too with hard work. This applies broadly—professionally, online, or in life. Others may only see the results, but you know your journey.

THOUGHTS

My Thoughts on "Having" to Educate Cisgender People

As a trans person, one of the challenges I face often is discussing transphobic remarks with cisgender people, only to hear them downplay it by saying, 'I don't think they meant that.' My perspective on being trans comes from lived experience, and I hope people respect that expertise. It's frustrating to deal with a lack of understanding on both sides, and it can feel like ignorance is being defended rather than addressed.

It's like, yeah, you don't want to think that other people are like that, that's really what you're saying. But a lot of people are transphobic, trying to play devil's advocate for things like that, when a trans person felt comfortable enough to discuss the incident with you that made them uncomfortable, and you've now made that trans person uncomfortable with you as well because you are actively trying not to understand why this is transphobic or why it has upset them. I always tell cisgender people, I don't want to teach you; teach yourselves on trans issues. I wasn't put on the earth to be every cisgender person's teacher that I come into contact with. Go out and educate yourselves, cisgender people. And when a trans person feels comfortable enough to talk to you about a situation that they feel strongly about, listen to their words. Really put yourself in their shoes and think if the thing that they want to hear is you defending something that they consider to be transphobic. As trans people, we weren't put on this earth to have to teach all the cisgender people to just be decent, kind human beings. And if nothing else, just treat people the way that you want to be treated.

Haters Are Fans

I woke up to a lot of transphobic hate on TikTok. My Google video got under a lot of people's skin. It's interesting when you're talking about a trans user experience that all people who respond to it in a hateful way are not trans people. Again, trying to make things on the internet about themselves that have nothing to do with them. When I worked in the adult industry, I got a lot of hate. I got death threats. I got doxxed. That's why I keep some things low-key. So once that starts to creep back in, I really don't particularly enjoy it. If I wanted to get a lot of visibility, I would be the person to get it.

I don't particularly enjoy attention because it's rarely positive; that said, I don't reciprocate on social media with traffic to trolls. You're welcome to look at the comments. They're quite vile. I appreciate all of the nice, lovely people that I interact with on a daily basis there. Believe me, it means a lot. I'm going to keep talking about trans issues, and if that pisses people off, that's their problem. I guarantee you all the comments are from incel accounts. They don't put their face out, they don't post videos, they don't say anything with their chest. Someone like me will always trigger the fuck out of someone like that who's so insecure that they can't even have their own online presence. Some of us in life are mirrors to people's other insecurities, and we trigger them because they're too weak to be who they truly are, and they hate on people who have confidence in themselves.

Why Pride Exists

We have Pride because of trans sex workers of color. You're gonna hear what I just said every Pride month, very performatively by a lot of white queer people, and then they're going to ignore trans sex workers of color and sex workers in general for the rest of the year. It's turned into a clickbait thing that white queer people say in the Summer, and it enrages me.

We have many trans surgery funds that say that they prioritize the most vulnerable of communities, yet never mention trans sex workers of color. We have many people in our community who will turn away people because they have worked in the adult industry. It is so hypocritical during Pride season if you are one of these people and you don't speak up for people's rights who are of one of the most marginalized and vulnerable communities. You benefit white people who are queer from trans sex workers of color. It all falls into white supremacy, and if you're not actively trying to dismantle that. What do you really have to be proud of? Something you have to ask yourself.

One month or one weekend of the year that you want to pop off and party, ask yourself what you are doing to contribute to enacting positive change and appreciating and acknowledging people, that if not for their actions, you would not benefit and enjoy Pride. My hope, coming from the adult entertainment community when I worked there and as a trans person, is to see that this is just a little thing. I want to see these nonprofits that cater to trans people say it, show it, be it on your site. Yes, we prioritize trans sex workers of color for our surgery funds, saying we prioritize helping and don't turn people away because we have some sort of internalized shame about the line of work that someone is in. People are more than their profession.

I would not have made it through the pandemic without the support of trans sex workers of color. Their help gave me access to resources and the confidence to be myself and speak up. If you're a white queer person, consider how you can contribute—not just during Pride, but throughout the year. If you're unsure, it's okay to ask. What matters is not turning a blind eye. Remember, real allyship is shown through consistent actions, not just words. Pride exists because of those who came before us—honor them by ensuring their continued visibility and support. Stand up, contribute, and make your allyship count every day.

You're Not an Ally

There was a TikTok video with a white cis straight woman saying she "needs a trans man to do the funniest thing ever" and go into the bathroom with a republican politician. For cisgender white women, understand this: that's not the take that you think it is. The white cishet woman is laughing the whole time, saying that she needs a trans man to do this. You need a trans man to go in and do something for you as a cis white straight woman so that you can laugh about it? You're not an ally because you don't actually have trans people in your life at all. We can tell, because that right there is something to laugh about to you. To make a mockery of us as trans men, for your own entertainment. That's not being an ally, that's being an asshole.

You're just as bad as the rest of them, but you don't realize it. You're not helping anyone. You're just making a mockery of trans men. And yeah, we are overlooked in a lot of the trans discussions because people want to demonize trans women so much, but this is not the take that you think it is in the comment section; it did not pass the vibe check either. I blocked this woman. And her ignorance. Thanks for putting that out there right after our Trans Day of Remembrance. Some of you still don't get it. It's not a joke. It's a right, a human right to be where we need to be, and we mind our own business and make jokes like this and make light of a situation that is difficult for all of us trans people. That's not you minding your business; that's not you being an ally. That's you trying to use our plight as transgender people for your cisgender entertainment. Think before you speak.

Trans Kids' Bodily Autonomy and My Experience as a Trans Man

When people know that I'm trans in the world, or even online, they always want to ask me what I think about health rights for trans kids. It's like cis people want to attempt to bait you as a trans person into these conversations, thinking that it will ever go in their favor is their biggest misstep.

What I always do is I share my personal story, because people are always looking for a reaction. But when you share a personal story, a personal experience, then it humanizes an issue, and they can see it from that perspective if they're not a trans person themselves. So, let's talk about my story. From a very young age, I knew that I was not the person people wanted to portray me as. I didn't want to wear the clothes my parents had chosen for me. I did not want to do the things that people wanted me to do. I wanted to do what I wanted to do because I wanted to be who I wanted to be. And I feel like that is a sign for a lot of us early on. That we're going to be trans, but we don't know, because again, I'm 41 years old, when I was young, people weren't talking about this.

I didn't have the tools, nor did my family have the knowledge of what it was to be a transgender person, but I always had the feeling that I didn't want to do what they were trying to make me do. I don't want to be who they're trying to make me be. The first instance of this. For decades, I struggled with suicide attempts and suicide ideation. I am no longer in that place because I am a happy trans man at this point in my life, but it took a lot for me to get there, and I went through a lot of unnecessary pain.

That's why I want to share my story: to help avoid as much unnecessary pain as possible for trans children. I hope this helps humanize us for cis people who may not be well educated about trans life experiences.

I knew I was different and struggling. The first time I saw a transgender character in the media was in Boys Don't Cry, when I was sixteen. I didn't want anyone to know I was curious about the topic. For those familiar with the movie, it's a hard story to see at that age. Immediately after watching, I didn't want to tell anyone how I felt, so for years, I tried to push it away.

I was plagued by depression and self-hatred, and then my body changed with puberty. With access to puberty blockers and relevant information before puberty, I could have avoided a body I didn't want, as well as surgeries later on. Education and medical options could have spared me a great deal of anguish.

When we break it down, it's really about education, right? The most effective way to humanize an issue is to educate people about it. So, by sharing my story, I hope this helps. Had puberty blockers been around when I was a child, it would have been something that I would have loved to have known about. People often bring up the topic of, 'Oh well, what if people change their minds?' Puberty blockers are just that. They block puberty. If you go off of them. You can go into puberty if you want to, or you can block them, and then you can pursue the avenues of transitioning if you so choose. However, that's the great thing about puberty blockers: they are reversible, as they act as a block. But puberty is not a block; it continues, and then later on, if you decide to go through surgeries, then you go through surgeries. But if you have puberty blockers, you can avoid that.

That would have been super helpful in my life. It would have saved me time, money, anguish, and a lot of pain and bad decisions that I made to reach the goal I needed to achieve, right? What the medical field and older trans people like me want is to make it better for the next generation of trans kids who don't have a voice and feel like they're stuck. We don't want them to feel like they're stuck. We don't want them to go through the pain that we've gone through. If it's avoidable, we want to help. And the best thing we can do by doing that is to use our voice. Share our stories and sign petitions.

Let's just think about ourselves at the end of the day, whether you're trans or not. You want bodily autonomy. My body, my choice. If there's a little kid, it's just as important. Their body, their choice, their voice needs to be heard if that's something that they are going through. It shouldn't just be taken away. It shouldn't just be written off. And it is a topic that needs to be put out more so that more people who are not trans can be educated on the experiences that we go through. Due to the major life challenges we face, we have a really high suicide rate. It's because our access to care is always under threat from people who are not trans, who are not listening to us, who are essentially saying our bodies are their choice. That's not acceptable.

Trans Rights & Trans Erasure Attempts

My main argument is that trans people deserve to be at the center of discussions about our own rights and issues, not sidelined or debated by cis people who have more media platform access. There is no legitimate debate about our humanity; trans people are people, deserving of rights like anyone else.

Referring to "the trans debate" is misleading; it is a manufactured controversy. We are people who deserve human rights like anyone else. The relentless discourse from cis people on trans issues is exhausting. More trans people should have opportunities to speak in the media on matters that directly impact us, not filtered through the perspectives of cis people. We are constantly subjected to debates about our existence by those outside our community. What makes you feel entitled to these pedestals? You shouldn't.

If we talk about the healthcare system, cis people mostly make decisions about health care that they have little firsthand knowledge of or education on. Trans people often have to teach cis people, making far-reaching decisions affecting our wellbeing. These decision-makers don't fully understand our situation, yet control our health and rights. Despite this, we rarely get to speak in the media, but hear cis people daily discuss 'the trans debate.'

The key point is that trans people, including those with uteruses, are regularly excluded from conversations about rights—even when those rights directly impact us. If cis people truly want to be allies, inviting trans voices into these discussions is essential. Our bodily autonomy and experiences should be included, not ignored.

So, yes, be an ally for us by speaking up, but also bring us in! Because it's not all about cis people dominating the conversation, I rarely ever see a trans person get interviewed on any news network, but we are talked about daily in numerous different ways. It starts to feel like even as allies, cis people don't quite get it because their job as an ally is to champion and bring people in. It's not to dominate the conversation.

Take out the word "transgender" from any title and replace it with any other characteristic, whether it be a race, religion, etc, and if that's how you need to understand how it's wrong to say "the trans debate", then that's how you need to understand it. At the end of the day, we're all human. We should all have the same rights. I want to hear from more people like me. I want to see more people who've gone through transitions be able to speak on our issues, and I don't want to hear it through some cis person's mouth, who is some host on a show whose heart's not in it, and they don't give a fuck.

My Thoughts on the 2024 US Election

I get quiet around elections. I have a lot on my mind. There's a lot on a lot of people's minds, but there's a lot on trans people's minds right now. Transitioning is the best thing I've done for my whole life, and every day, there's someone who won't speak up for you, there's someone who'll speak against you.

There's a lot of that going around. Therefore, there are feelings of anxiety, despair, uncertainty, and disappointment. They're amplified in these election seasons with these politicians because it's extremely hard to live as a trans person in the United States, to have your identity be politicized, and to never necessarily have candidates really stand on business and say it when they're asked if they'll treat us as equals.

I'm disappointed in the current system. I intentionally say "cis-tem," emphasizing how it's structured to benefit cis people while often leaving out trans people. Our bodies and rights are frequently politicized, and even those running for office sometimes avoid openly supporting us as equal citizens. So, am I looking forward to this election? Not really, but that's my personal experience. I've worked hard to be who I am, and while I'm grateful and happy for the life I have now, I do have concerns about the future.

Cis Men Stop Doing This, It's Weird

Cis men, stop centering yourself in my online comment sections on my story time videos, for those of you who don't know. When I share a story time of my life as a trans man, as a trans experience, and you decide as a cis man to go to my comments section and say I've never experienced that. That's never happened to me. This is about, and then just go off about yourself. Yeah. The whole video was about my experience as a trans person. Not a welcome in for you to center the conversation around yourself. It's literally me sharing a life story about my trans experience as a trans man. Of course, you would not have that. You're a cis man.

Lush: An Exemplary Authentic Execution of Corporate Social Responsibility and Allyship

The best and most authentic execution of corporate social responsibility and allyship that I have ever experienced in a brand was at Lush. I was really excited to go with my boyfriend. We were going to get the Ninja Turtle bath bombs. I needed something to cheer me up. We walked in, we saw the display, we were excited, and we were greeted by the nice people at Lush. We walk up to the register, and as we wait in line, I see a booklet. It said "support trans people, a guide to turning allyship into action".

As a trans person, that hit me hard—I was overcome by a positive shock of feeling supported, welcome, and safe. For a business to stand so openly behind allyship was something new to me. I even pointed it out to my boyfriend, who was hardly able to process my emotions. As we checked out, I tried not to cry, but when I spoke to the lady at the register, I couldn't hold back my tears. It meant a great deal because we rarely experience happy surprises like this. Rather than a marketing gimmick, this booklet, co-written with the National Center for Transgender Equality, truly showed authentic allyship. The staff, especially the manager, expressed genuine love for how Lush operates and their values.

So, we're getting rung up, start talking, and I knew I was like, don't cry, don't cry, don't cry. And the second we started talking to the lady who was checking us out, I lost it and started crying. I was like, this means so much as a trans person because we never have happy surprises. I haven't had a happy surprise like this anywhere, but not even from a business for a business to just hold that space and not turn it into a full-blown marketing campaign and like gimmick, but to truly be an ally and have this whole booklet there that they co-wrote with the National Center for Transgender Equality is amazing. It was an amazing experience for me. She was incredibly nice. I believe she was the store manager. She told me she had been working for Lush for a really long time and that's why she stays there, it's because she truly loves how the business is run, and their values.

I think I will always be a fan of Lush. I was a fan before, but I will not shut up about Lush now. Lush is an authentic ally. As a trans man, I have never experienced this in any other business. You know, I have gone through a lot of the hard things in terms of business and discrimination for being trans, and so this booklet at Lush was something that I could never dream of seeing. You can't quantify the impact that this will have, but it is huge.

Transitioning FTM Focused Products I've Used and my Thoughts

Transitioning is expensive! I have spent a significant amount of money on items throughout this transition that I didn't use, didn't work out, and weren't really in my best interest. I don't know. Here are a few of the things, right, like I was going back and forth with. The packing, right, and all that stuff, and I spent so much money on something like this one, which was a 3-in-1. It was like an STP you could use in the bedroom and a pack, right? And so, I spent about $500 on it. Didn't line up well with my body, nonrefundable because it's a personal item. In the bedroom, it's not super comfortable or pleasurable. And, in terms of packing, what I realized is that I don't enjoy it. The only reason I will ever pack is if I need it for an underwear modeling job.

In my day-to-day, I don't use it. I don't have that dysphoria, you know, we're all different in that way. And then there are all the self-care products, right? And so. I'm fortunate enough to have been testing out a lot of products that have been given to me, but what I'm learning is that the beard is my thing right now. I'm trying a derma roller, as well as various types of beard growth serums, oils, and other products.

Today, I think I overdid it because my voice felt a little scratchy, and it's because I overused a new biotin serum or some other beard growth product. Even this far along in my transition, I can overthink it, and my body is just telling me to chill out. So that's what I'm gonna do with the beard right now. I'm going to appreciate what I have because it's taken me quite a while to get there, and even if it doesn't come in fully. It's still cool. It's much the same way I viewed my top surgery, too. It's not perfect, but I love it.

Moving Thoughts

Looking back on the apartment I've lived in for the last four years (June 2020 - September 2024), I recall feeling excited to move in during the pandemic, expecting it to be temporary. Yet, I stayed four years—easily the most challenging of my life. During that time, I experienced a brief burst of fame, flew out for top surgery, met some wonderful people, and eventually met my boyfriend. Now, we've moved in together!

It's interesting to observe the growth that occurs in the chaos of my life, particularly with my Gemini sun, as I'm a Capricorn rising and an Aries Moon. So that makes for quite the dynamic on top of everything else. There were moments of great sorrow in that little room, and there were moments of great happiness too. On the days I hated living there, I knew I would leave at some point, and on the days when things worked out, it gave me hope. I did love West Hollywood to a certain extent. I would never live there again. I'm not in a partying place in my life. It served me well when I was much younger. It's just not my vibe anymore.

CLOSING

I've shared glimpses into my life story in the hopes that, in some way, it's either helped you as a trans person yourself or, if you are cisgender that I've humanized a transgender person's existence and that you now have a deeper understanding of some of the challenges we as transgender people may face and can now hopefully be kinder towards us.

For those in the entertainment industry, with the means, please reach out. Let's turn my book into a series. I can be reached at info@cotterthecreative.com - that's show business.